CPSIA information can be obtained
at www.ICGtesting.com
Printed in the USA
BVHW011209240323
661080BV00015B/691

9 781953 829467

הגדה מן המצר

Haggadah
Min HaMeitzar
From the Narrows

Gabriella Spitzer

Ben Yehuda Press
Teaneck, New Jersey

Published by Ben Yehuda Press
122 Ayers Court #1B
Teaneck, NJ 07666
http://www.BenYehudaPress.com

To subscribe to our monthly book club and support independent Jewish publishing, visit https://www.patreon.com/BenYehudaPress

Ben Yehuda Press books may be purchased at a discount by synagogues, book clubs, and other institutions buying in bulk.

For information, please email markets@BenYehudaPress.com

ISBN13 978-1-953829-46-7

23 24 25 / 10 9 8 7 6 5 4 3 2   20230220

Our tradition, like the Torah scroll itself, is a vast collection of points of light; an accumulation of revelation, wisdom, lived experience, trial and error, conversation, disagreement. Like the experience of stargazing, seeking a way into Jewish tradition can feel awe-inspiring and transcendent; can feel cozy and comforting; can feel overwhelming and even infuriating.

We each, as individuals embedded in families and communities, find our own tools for navigating the tradition. We choose which parts we want to become intimate with. We both inherit and choose the maps that orient us. We grow up in and learn new languages that unlock doors to collective memory and meaning-making. Lineage and identity shape what we are given access to; we find our way out of traditions that are stifling, and across barriers that seem impenetrable.

Rabbi Leora Abelson
Yom Kippur 5783
Nehar Shalom Community Synagogue

Introduction

This Haggadah was born of a desire to provide a new tool for navigating the tradition. The seder can be awe-inspiring and transcendent, cozy and comforting, overwhelming and infuriating. This Haggadah does not hide the beauty or the challenges in our tradition. Instead, it provides commentary and perspectives to help us all find new meaning (and maybe new challenges), year after year.

The Jewish tradition is inherently multivocal and multilayered. The Haggadah is no exception. It was compiled over the last 1500 years or so, and it tells a story that is much older. Yet that is also a simplification. The Haggadah tells the story of the Exodus, and it insists it is a timeless story. We must see ourselves in it. To help, the Haggadah provides stories of previous generations telling the story. We should see ourselves not simply as inheritors of a story, but of a tradition and a chain.

However, too frequently many of us don't see ourselves represented in the tradition. The tradition has been written and codified largely by straight cis men. Women's voices and queer voices have been suppressed if not outright ignored. But our ancestors, too, were slaves in Egypt and have suffered in restricted circumstances throughout history. Whether or not any given Haggadah mentions it, the Seder tells a queer story.

Further, that queerness is inherent in the tradition. As Laynie Solomon, Associate Rosh Yeshiva of SVARA, writes:

Halakhic discourse and practice is not about reifying a binary of yes or no; it is about creating space for clarity and authenticity in each moment of messy gradational life. Non-binary ways of thinking allow us to restore aspects of halakha that have been ignored for far too long. This isn't a reimagining of halakha—this is halakha.

Similarly, the queerness of the Passover seder is not new or imposed. The Passover story has always been about the clarity, authenticity, and messiness inherent in discussions of freedom, liberation, and oppression. This Haggadah does not reflect a reimagining of the Passover seder—it is the Passover seder.

Haggadah Min HaMeitzar aims to bring that vision forward. The Haggadah text it uses is almost entirely traditional. There are very few omissions[1] and only a couple of additions/changes.[2] However, the commentary is entirely original. It provides quotations, questions, and prompts inspired by rabbinic, queer, Indigenous, feminist, environmental and other sources. I hope you find the commentary provokes deep discussion and meaningful debates at your seders.

---

[1] The math section about the number of plagues is missing.

[2] Miriam's cup is a recent addition. Rabban Gamliel's commentary on pesach, matzah, and maror have been moved from Maggid to the Korech, Motzei Matzah, and Maror sections. There are also a couple points in Maggid where the traditional midrash has been slightly adjusted.

Tips For Those Leading Seders

There are many ways to experience the seder—even at the same seder. All are okay...as long as everyone is able to choose their path.

Consider this scenario: A dozen members of the extended Cardozo family have assembled for Passover. They are deep in the midrash section of Maggid. Six members of the family are in the living room, vigorously discussing Shifra and Puah's civil disobedience and how it is still relevant today. Two other members of the family are in the living room, too. One is reading another commentary from earlier in the seder, and another is quietly absorbing the discussion. Two family members are in the kitchen, seasoning the soup and discussing the menu. The others are running around searching for the afikoman.

Who, among the Cardozos, is engaged in the seder? They all are. It's easy as a seder leader to feel like everyone must be part of the discussion or in the same room or on the same page. Relax—one of the beauties of the seder tradition is that there are so many ways to engage and to find meaning.

However! Everyone should be able to choose how they engage themselves. Consider the pair in the kitchen. What demographics do you imagine? Make sure folks who fit those demographics (or the person in your family who always cooks, or always hosts) is able to engage

as they please. Plan ahead, and confirm each year who wants to have which roles. To the extent that it is possible, plan food that does not need encouragement during Maggid so everyone who wants to remain in the discussion can do so.

Plan two distinct seders (if that's your practice).

Most Jews outside of Israel hold two Passover seders. If you plan two seders, plan different guest lists and different approaches. Maybe in the first seder, you want to make sure to recite the entire Haggadah, but in the second seder, you want to focus on a few key elements. Maybe in the first seder, you want to focus on the storytelling theme, and focus on the environmental theme in the second seder.

This Haggadah is designed to be used at many, many seders over many years, and have no two seders alike. I hope you find it to work that way!

Pick two of three: short, comprehensive, and/or in depth.

You can have a seder that lasts only a couple hours. You can have a seder that covers every word in the Haggadah. You can have a seder that has deep, thoughtful conversations on meaningful topics. You cannot expect all three at

the same seder.[1]

So pick your priorities ahead of time. If you know you want to get to dinner before 11, decide in advance what you plan to skip and what you want to emphasize. If you want meaningful conversations, think ahead about what questions you want to pose or what themes you want to probe. This Haggadah makes themes easy: consider choosing one voice to follow throughout your seder. If you want to recite every word (but not be up until dawn like the five rabbis discussed in Maggid), practice cutting off the conversation: "that's a great conversation—why don't you continue it over dinner, when we get there" should work nicely.

Eat a large salad course for karpas—and keep eating!

Erev Pesach—the day when seder is that night—can be busy and stressful. It often does not involve full or regular meals. Our kitchens are all mixed up, with no more chametz, but also a strong custom to forgo any matzah until seder. There's a lot of work to do, especially if you are hosting. Traveling can also throw off our systems. Many people start seder feeling a little bit "off." If this is you—don't despair!

There is a misguided tradition to stay hungry throughout the seder to make the first taste of matzah that much more sweet. I do not recommend this custom. Instead, I recommend serving a full karpas course with lots of roasted and raw vegetables and lots of dips. Consider roasted potatoes with garlic aioli, roasted beets with almondaise, and/or artichokes with pesto. Make it substantial, especially if you anticipate a long Maggid. Keep the snacks coming throughout Maggid. It is easier to make meaning when you're not uncomfortably hungry.

Focus on the big picture: This is the holiday of freedom.

Several of my friends have shared that they approach Passover with more dread than excitement. Even if you aren't hosting a seder, Passover can be a lot of work! Changing kitchens over, traveling, and taking time off work can all be hard and stressful. Our Christian-centric society does not make things easier. However, this is the holiday of freedom. Focus on the big picture and what will bring meaning.

---

[1] In 2020 and 2021, my partner and I made seder by ourselves to avoid spreading COVID-19. It turned out that our seders with only two people (both highly knowledgeable of the seder text) ended before midnight, covered nearly the entire text, and had meaningful conversations. If you're planning a very small seder, you might have a similar experience! But don't count on it.

Using Haggadah Min Hameitzar

בֶּן בַּג בַּג אוֹמֵר, הֲפֹךְ בָּה וַהֲפֹךְ בָּה, דְכֹלָא בָה.

Ben Bag Bag said, "Turn it and turn it, because everything is in it." (Pirkei Avot 5:22)

Every Passover, we return to the same rituals and stories. And every Passover is different because every year, we are different. The seder provides countless opportunities to find meaning, challenge, and discussion. Every year, as we find ourselves at the seder table, we should find new questions and have new conversations.

Haggadah Min HaMeitzar is designed to help you find new questions, discussion topics, and insights, year after year. it uses a full, traditional text, paired with original commentary in four voices. The art found throughout the Haggadah forms another layer of commentary for discussion and analysis.

There are many ways to use the Haggadah, from planning carefully which commentaries and art to discuss to letting the conversation develop organically. However, here are some ideas:

- **Themed seder:** Focus on one voice for your seder. Read the commentaries in one color. Discuss the text and the art from that lens.

- **Each person focuses on one voice:** Assign each seder participant one voice as their focus. One or two people can each represent the environmental, embodiment, storytelling, and liberation voices.

- **Art seder:** Focus on the art as commentary. What speaks to you? How does the art respond to the Haggadah text? To the themes of the seder?

- **Min HaMeitzar:** "Meitzar" means narrow place. It is also related to the word Mitzrayim (Egypt). This is a theme throughout the Haggadah. How does the text in different parts of the seder relate to coming out of narrow spaces? How does the art reflect this theme? What does it mean to you, this year?

A Note On Texts And Translations

Haggadah Min HaMeitzar was built from the Ashkenazi Haggadah text from Sefaria.com. The Hebrew text has been modified (other than for cosmetic changes) only where noted. The translation has been edited for clarity and emphasis. We also removed gendered references to God. Jewish tradition, and the Hebrew Haggadah text, have historically used masculine pronouns and imagery to refer to God. However, Jewish tradition also reminds us of the limitations of humanity in comprehending the divine. God's pronoun is God.

The Four Voices Of The Commentary

Haggadah Min HaMeitzar is traditional and progressive. Its original commentary is presented in four voices corresponding to the four names of the holiday. Each voice has a corresponding color and icon for clarity.

- Chag HaCheirut: Passover is about liberation and redemption from oppression, a theme that is still deeply relevant today.

- Chag HaMatzot: Passover is an embodied holiday. The seder is not solely an intellectual exercise. These sources emphasize the aspects of the ritual that are touched and tasted.

- Chag HaAviv: Passover is the springtime holiday. We read Song of Songs. This voice shares naturalist sources and Torah from the earth.

- Chag HaPesach: At the seder, we tell a story about telling a story. Everything is new in each generation, and we are tied to every previous generation before us, both in what they said in how they said it. This commentary provides a connection to how we have told our foundational stories over time.

Each voice includes brief sources from activists, scientists, poets, and others; thought-provoking discussion questions; and commentary from the rabbinic tradition through the ages.

Art In Haggadah Min Hameitzar

The art in Haggadah Min HaMeitzar is designed to provide another type of commentary and insight into the seder. There are a wide variety of media, including acrylics on canvas, silk paint on silk, digital art, watercolors, mixed media, and more. Here are a few questions to prompt discussions of the art.

- How does this piece comment on the text — the themes of liberation, embodiment, environmentalism, and/or storytelling?
- How does this piece speak to you?

What do you notice first? What feels challenging or interesting?

- What does the choice of medium add to the message of the art?
- Haggadot are a rare source of illumination and art throughout Jewish history. Do any of the pieces in Haggadah Min HaMeitzar seem inspired by those traditions?

The art is all original and created for the Haggadah by Gabriella Spitzer. More details can be found on page 118.

Preparing For Passover:
Bedikat Chameitz/Search For Chameitz

Leading up to Passover, we clean our houses to be free of chameitz (leavened foods). This process culminates with the search for chameitz the night before Passover. (When Passover starts on Saturday night, the search is completed on Thursday night.)

It is traditional to save out a set number of pieces of bread, crackers, or pasta. Hide these around your house. Then search for all chameitz (not just what you hid!) using the light of a candle. It is traditional to use a feather or spoon to aid in the search and collection.

Before the search, recite:

Blessed are You, Lord our God, Ruler of the Universe, who blessed us with commandments and obligated us to remove all chameitz.

בָּרוּךְ אַתָּה יהוה, אֱלֹהֵינוּ מֶלֶךְ הָעוֹלָם, אֲשֶׁר קִדְּשָׁנוּ בְּמִצְוֹתָיו וְצִוָּנוּ עַל בְּעוּר חָמֵץ.

Search for the chameitz. After the search, recite:

All chameitz under my jurisdiction, which I have not seen and removed, or of which I am unaware, is hereby nullified and ownerless as the dust of the earth.

כָּל חֲמִירָא וַחֲמִיעָא דְּאִכָּא בִרְשׁוּתִי, דְּלָא חֲמִתֵהּ וּדְלָא בְעַרְתֵהּ וּדְלָא יְדַעְנָא לֵהּ, לִבָּטֵל וְלֶהֱוֵי הֶפְקֵר כְּעַפְרָא דְּאַרְעָא.

Save the chameitz until the next morning.

The following morning, take the chameitz from the search as well as any other leftover chameitz from breakfast or otherwise. Burn it, compost it, or otherwise throw it out. Then say:

All chameitz under my jurisdiction, whether I have seen it or not, whether I have removed it or not, is hereby nullified and ownerless as the dust of the earth.

כָּל חֲמִירָא וַחֲמִיעָא דְּאִכָּא בִרְשׁוּתִי, דַּחֲזִתֵּהּ וּדְלָא חֲזִתֵּהּ, דַּחֲמִתֵּהּ וּדְלָא חֲמִתֵּהּ, דְּבִעַרְתֵּהּ וּדְלָא בִעַרְתֵּהּ, לִבָּטֵל וְלֶהֱוֵי הֶפְקֵר כְּעַפְרָא דְאַרְעָא.

Spiritual Chameitz

Many Jewish thinkers have discussed the spiritual side of chameitz. What is "puffy" or overly showy about ourselves? What gets in the way of serving our communities and God most effectively? What would it mean to search our interior selves with a candle? How can we recommit to pursuing liberation this year?

Preparing For Passover: Setting The Table

The Passover table is full of ritual foods and items that serve as props and prompts for discussion throughout the seder. Set the seder plate with the following ritual foods. There are many ways to prepare them, and they hold many layers of meaning.

Roasted egg (*beitzah*)
Hardboil an egg and let it dry completely. Light a candle. Grasp the sides of the egg and carefully move it through the candle flame so it creates streaks of soot on the surface of the shell. Repeat to create several streaks. The egg on the seder plate is typically not consumed. The egg symbolizes springtime and cycles. It also symbolizes the Passover offering in the time of the Temple.

Shankbone or beet (*zeroah*)
Roast a shankbone or beet. The shankbone or beet on the seder plate is typically not consumed.
The shankbone or beet symbolizes the Passover offering in the time of the Temple. The shankbone also symbolizes God's outstretched arm.

Bitter herbs (*maror/chazeret*)
Traditional bitter herbs include horseradish root and bitter lettuce.
The bitter herbs symbolize the bitterness of the oppression in Egypt.

Charoset
Charoset is a sweet paste or a spread. Recipes differ across the world, but they typically include dates, nuts, apples, cinnamon, and/or wine. A thick charoset made out of dates or other dried fruit can be shaped into a pyramid to be deconstructed during the seder.
The charoset symbolizes the apple trees where the enslaved Israelites in Egypt would spent romantic time together (see midrash on page 42). It also symbolizes the mortar of the bricks the Israelites made as slaves.

Springtime herbs (*karpas*)
Traditional karpas foods include parsley and potatoes. They are dipped in saltwater.
The springtime herbs symbolize spring. The saltwater represents the Israelite's tears.

Blood orange (*tapuz*)
Cut a blood orange in half and place on the seder plate. The blood orange is typically not consumed, but it is referenced in the b'damayich chayee passage (page 37).
The orange is a newer addition to the seder plate to symbolize fights for liberation for the queer community. Use a blood orange to represent the blood, sweat, and tears needed in the fight for liberation.

Matzah
Place three sheets of matzah on a plate or holder on the table and cover them.
The matzah represents the bread of destitution eaten as the Israelites left Egypt.

Egg

Shankbone
or Beet

Blood Orange

Bitter Herbs

Springtime Herbs

Charoset

Matzah

Order Of The Seder

קַדֵּשׁ

וּרְחַץ

כַּרְפַּס

יַחַץ

מַגִּיד

רָחְצָה

מוֹצִיא מַצָּה

מָרוֹר

כּוֹרֵךְ

צָפוּן

בָּרֵךְ

הַלֵּל

נִרְצָה

Kiddush   קַדֵּשׁ

Fill the first cup of wine.

On Shabbat, start here:

There was evening and there was
morning, the sixth day. The heaven
and the earth were finished, and all
their host. And on the seventh day
God finished the work God had done;
and rested on the seventh day from
all the work which God had done.
And God blessed the seventh day,
and sanctified it; because God rested
on it from all of the work which God
created in doing.

וַיְהִי עֶרֶב וַיְהִי בֹקֶר יוֹם הַשִּׁשִּׁי.
וַיְכֻלּוּ הַשָּׁמַיִם וְהָאָרֶץ וְכָל־צְבָאָם.
וַיְכַל אֱלֹהִים בַּיּוֹם הַשְּׁבִיעִי
מְלַאכְתּוֹ אֲשֶׁר עָשָׂה וַיִּשְׁבֹּת בַּיּוֹם
הַשְּׁבִיעִי מִכָּל מְלַאכְתּוֹ אֲשֶׁר
עָשָׂה. וַיְבָרֶךְ אֱלֹהִים אֶת יוֹם
הַשְּׁבִיעִי וַיְקַדֵּשׁ אוֹתוֹ כִּי בוֹ שָׁבַת
מִכָּל־מְלַאכְתּוֹ אֲשֶׁר בָּרָא אֱלֹהִים
לַעֲשׂוֹת.

On weekdays, start here. Inclusions for Shabbat are in brackets.

Blessed are You, our God, Ruler of
the universe, who grows the fruit of the
vine. Blessed are You, our God, Ruler of
the universe, who has chosen us from all
peoples, raised us above all languages, and
sanctified us with Your commandments.
And You have given us, Lord our God,
[Shabbat for rest], regular times for
happiness, holidays and special times for
joy, [this Shabbat day, and] this Festival
of Matzot, our season of freedom [in
love] a holy convocation in memory of the
Exodus from Egypt. For You have chosen
us and sanctified us above all peoples. In
Your gracious love, You granted us Your
[holy Shabbat, and] special times for
happiness and joy. Blessed are You, our
God, Ruler of the universe, who makes
[Shabbat], Israel, and holidays holy.

בָּרוּךְ אַתָּה יהוה, אֱלֹהֵינוּ מֶלֶךְ
הָעוֹלָם בּוֹרֵא פְּרִי הַגָּפֶן.
בָּרוּךְ אַתָּה יהוה, אֱלֹהֵינוּ מֶלֶךְ
הָעוֹלָם אֲשֶׁר בָּחַר בָּנוּ מִכָּל־עָם
וְרוֹמְמָנוּ מִכָּל־לָשׁוֹן וְקִדְּשָׁנוּ בְּמִצְוֹתָיו.
וַתִּתֶּן לָנוּ יהוה אֱלֹהֵינוּ בְּאַהֲבָה
[שַׁבָּתוֹת לִמְנוּחָה וּ] מוֹעֲדִים לְשִׂמְחָה,
חַגִּים וּזְמַנִּים לְשָׂשׂוֹן, [אֶת יוֹם הַשַּׁבָּת
הַזֶּה וְ] אֶת יוֹם חַג הַמַּצּוֹת הַזֶּה זְמַן
חֵרוּתֵנוּ, [בְּאַהֲבָה] מִקְרָא קֹדֶשׁ זֵכֶר
לִיצִיאַת מִצְרָיִם. כִּי בָנוּ בָחַרְתָּ וְאוֹתָנוּ
קִדַּשְׁתָּ מִכָּל הָעַמִּים, [וְשַׁבָּת] וּמוֹעֲדֵי
קָדְשֶׁךָ [בְּאַהֲבָה וּבְרָצוֹן] בְּשִׂמְחָה
וּבְשָׂשׂוֹן הִנְחַלְתָּנוּ.
בָּרוּךְ אַתָּה יהוה, מְקַדֵּשׁ [הַשַּׁבָּת וְ]
יִשְׂרָאֵל וְהַזְּמַנִּים.

On Saturday evening, add this paragraph.

A Distinction Between Holy And Holy

This is an extraordinary blessing. We are marking the transition from Shabbat-holiness to Passover-holiness. What does it mean to differentiate between holy and holy?

Blessed are You, our God, Ruler of the universe, who creates the light of the fire. Blessed are You, our God, Ruler of the universe, who distinguishes between the holy and the profane, between light and darkness, between Israel and the nations, between the seventh day and the six working days. You have distinguished between the holiness of the Shabbat and the holiness of the Festival, and You have sanctified the seventh day above the six working days. You have distinguished and sanctified Your people Israel with Your holiness.

Blessed are You, our God, Ruler of the universe, who distinguishes between holy and holy.

בָּרוּךְ אַתָּה יהוה, אֱלֹהֵינוּ מֶלֶךְ הָעוֹלָם, בּוֹרֵא מְאוֹרֵי הָאֵשׁ. בָּרוּךְ אַתָּה יהוה, אֱלֹהֵינוּ מֶלֶךְ הָעוֹלָם הַמַּבְדִּיל בֵּין קֹדֶשׁ לְחֹל, בֵּין אוֹר לְחֹשֶׁךְ, בֵּין יִשְׂרָאֵל לָעַמִּים, בֵּין יוֹם הַשְּׁבִיעִי לְשֵׁשֶׁת יְמֵי הַמַּעֲשֶׂה. בֵּין קְדֻשַּׁת שַׁבָּת לִקְדֻשַּׁת יוֹם טוֹב הִבְדַּלְתָּ, וְאֶת־יוֹם הַשְּׁבִיעִי מִשֵּׁשֶׁת יְמֵי הַמַּעֲשֶׂה קִדַּשְׁתָּ. הִבְדַּלְתָּ וְקִדַּשְׁתָּ אֶת־עַמְּךָ יִשְׂרָאֵל בִּקְדֻשָּׁתֶךָ. בָּרוּךְ אַתָּה יהוה, הַמַּבְדִּיל בֵּין קֹדֶשׁ לְקֹדֶשׁ.

Who Helps Us Grow And Thrive And Brings Us To This Day

Think back to this time last year. Where were you? What was your seder like? Where are you now? What has changed? What has stayed the same? How have you grown this past year?

Continue here (all days).

Blessed are You, our God, Ruler of the universe, who helps us grow and thrive and brings us to this day.

בָּרוּךְ אַתָּה יהוה, אֱלֹהֵינוּ מֶלֶךְ הָעוֹלָם, שֶׁהֶחֱיָנוּ וְקִיְּמָנוּ וְהִגִּיעָנוּ לַזְּמַן הַזֶּה.

It is traditional to drink while leaning to the left to symbolize our freedom and ability to enjoy a leisurely meal.

 *Chag HaAviv* Environmental

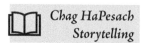 *Chag HaPesach* Storytelling

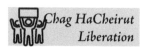 *Chag HaCheirut* Liberation

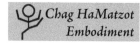 *Chag HaMatzot* Embodiment

The four cups have many meanings. The first cup focuses on the four seasons.

First Cup: The Four Seasons

כִּי־הִנֵּה הַסְּתָו עָבָר הַגֶּשֶׁם חָלַף הָלַךְ לוֹ. הַנִּצָּנִים נִרְאוּ בָאָרֶץ עֵת הַזָּמִיר הִגִּיעַ וְקוֹל הַתּוֹר נִשְׁמַע בְּאַרְצֵנוּ.

For now the winter is past; the rains are over and gone. The buds have appeared in the land; the time of singing has come; the song of the turtledove is heard in our land. (Song of Songs 2:11-12)

According to Shir HaShirim Rabbah, a collection of midrash on Song of Songs, the "winter" refers to the 400 years of slavery in Egypt, and the winter ending refers to the Exodus. The "buds" refer to the leaders who brought the people out, and the "song" refers to the song at the Red Sea.

As we begin the journey from slavery to freedom tonight, what are you leaving in the winter? What song will you sing in freedom?

Handwashing

Wash hands without saying a blessing.

Water: A Source Of Life And Vulnerability

We wash our hands in fresh water and then dip our vegetables in salt water. The salt water is symbolic of the tears our ancestors shed while they were oppressed in Egypt and throughout history. It also reminds us of the ocean, the origin of all life.

Water is a theme throughout the seder. Our ancestors walked through the split water, the birth canal, to leave Egypt and emerge as a new, free people. Miriam's well of water nourished the people of Israel during their wanderings in the desert. However, water can be a source of pain and vulnerability. Pharaoh commands that Israelite baby boys be thrown in the Nile. Later, God turns the Nile to blood, killing all the fish and polluting the entire ecosystem.

Water is not just a symbol. It is a material, essential for life. Today, as in Egypt, our rivers and other fresh water sources are vulnerable to violence, greed, and pollution. The salt water reminds us of this fragility and vulnerability. Salt water is part of our stories and our bodies. It is the origin of all life in the ocean. Yet we cannot drink it, and on land, it too pollutes.

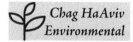
Chag HaAviv
Environmental

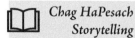
Chag HaPesach
Storytelling

Chag HaCheirut
Liberation

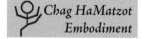
Chag HaMatzot
Embodiment

Karpas

כַּרְפַּס

Take a small portion of greens or root vegetables (parsley and potatoes are both traditional) and dip them into salt water. Say the blessing before eating.

בָּרוּךְ אַתָּה יהוה, אֱלֹהֵינוּ מֶלֶךְ הָעוֹלָם, בּוֹרֵא פְּרִי הָאֲדָמָה.

Blessed are you, Lord our God, Ruler of the universe,
  who creates the fruit of the earth.

From Freshwater To Ocean

Each day for a hundred days I have walked to the water's edge and greeted it: "Hello sea!" I have offered my jar up to the wave and caught one. Perhaps this will help, I think, taking the sea home with me. A magical place might be able to cast magical spells. I take each jar home and store it carefully on the shelves of my glass-fronted bookcase. Shelves fill as I number each jar with a luggage tag—noting the day and time of the wave's capture. How many to replace the water in my body? Another 300? A transfusion, not of blood, but of saline—from freshwater to ocean.

—Louise Kenward, from "Searching for Seahorses" in *Women on Nature*

Break

Remove the middle matzah from its holder. Break it in half.
Place the larger half aside to become the afikoman and return the smaller piece. Hide the afikoman.

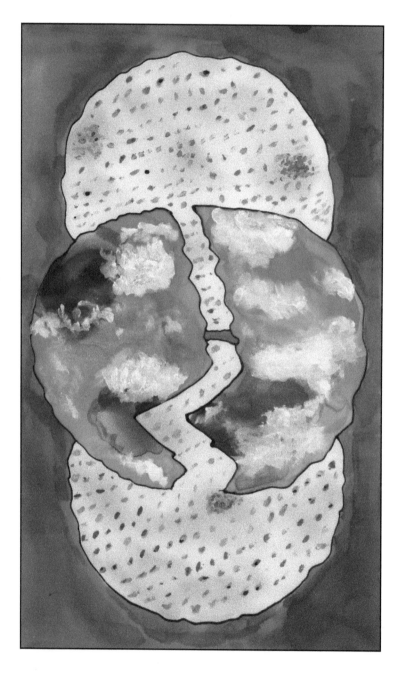

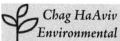 *Chag HaAviv*
Environmental

 *Chag HaPesach*
Storytelling

 *Chag HaCheirut*
Liberation

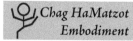 *Chag HaMatzot*
Embodiment

Storytelling

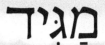

Matzah, the bread of hospitality

The Maggid/Storytelling section begins with the matzah and an invitation for anyone to come join in the seder.

Uncover the matzah and point to it.

This is the bread of destitution that our ancestors ate in the land of Egypt.

הָא לַחְמָא עַנְיָא דִּי אֲכָלוּ
אַבְהָתָנָא בְּאַרְעָא דְמִצְרָיִם.

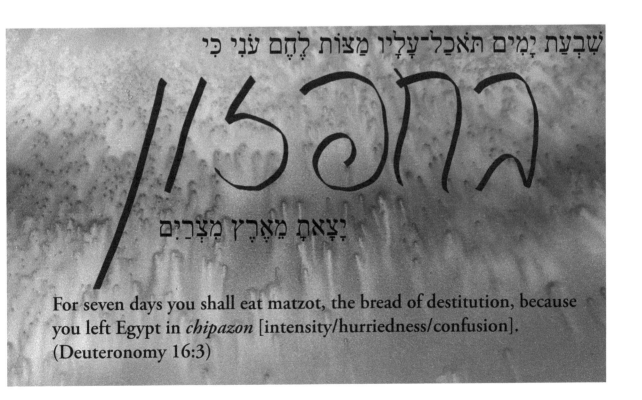

שִׁבְעַת יָמִים תֹּאכַל־עָלָיו מַצּוֹת לֶחֶם עֹנִי כִּי

יְצָאתָ מֵאֶרֶץ מִצְרַיִם

For seven days you shall eat matzot, the bread of destitution, because you left Egypt in *chipazon* [intensity/hurriedness/confusion]. (Deuteronomy 16:3)

Anyone who is hungry should come and eat, anyone who is in need should come and share Pesach with us.

Now we are here, next year we will be in the land of Israel. This year we are slaves, next year we will be free people.

כָּל דִּכְפִין יֵיתֵי וְיֵיכֹל, כָּל דִּצְרִיךְ יֵיתֵי וְיִפְסַח. הָשַׁתָּא הָכָא, לְשָׁנָה הַבָּאָה בְּאַרְעָא דְיִשְׂרָאֵל. הָשַׁתָּא עַבְדֵי, לְשָׁנָה הַבָּאָה בְּנֵי חוֹרִין.

All Flourishing Is Mutual

Forest ecologists hypothesize mast fruiting [synchronized fruiting at irregular intervals] is the simple outcome of this energetic equation: make fruit only when you can afford it... If this were true, each tree would fruit on its own schedule, predictable by the size of its reserves of stored starch. But they don't. If one tree fruits, they all fruit— there are no soloists. Not one tree in a grove, but the whole grove; not one grove in the forest, but every grove; all across the county and all across the state. The trees act not as individuals, but somehow as a collective. Exactly how they do this, we don't yet know. But what we see is the power of unity. What happens to one happens to all us all. We can starve together or feast together. All flourishing is mutual.

—Robin Wall Kimmerer, *Braiding Sweetgrass*

Bread Of Affliction Or Bread Of Liberation?

We eat the matzah to embody the intense experience of leaving Egypt.
Even so, there is a fundamental tension within the matzah.
Is it lechem oni, the bread of affliction, or is it the bread of liberation?
What do we learn from it being both?

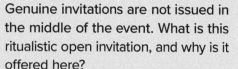

Genuine invitations are not issued in the middle of the event. What is this ritualistic open invitation, and why is it offered here?

What is the relationship between poverty/hunger and freedom?

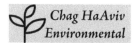 *Chag HaAviv* **Environmental**

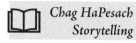 *Chag HaPesach* **Storytelling**

 *Chag HaCheirut* **Liberation**

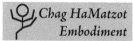 *Chag HaMatzot* **Embodiment**

A Special Night

The seder is a special meal with special foods and rituals. We now ask four questions (really, one question with four answers) that highlight the differences between tonight and every other night.

It is traditional for the youngest participant at the seder to share the four questions.

מַה נִּשְׁתַּנָּה הַלַּיְלָה הַזֶּה מִכָּל הַלֵּילוֹת?
שֶׁבְּכָל הַלֵּילוֹת אָנוּ אוֹכְלִין חָמֵץ וּמַצָּה, הַלַּיְלָה הַזֶּה - כֻּלּוֹ מַצָּה.
שֶׁבְּכָל הַלֵּילוֹת אָנוּ אוֹכְלִין שְׁאָר יְרָקוֹת - הַלַּיְלָה הַזֶּה מָרוֹר.
שֶׁבְּכָל הַלֵּילוֹת אֵין אָנוּ מַטְבִּילִין אֲפִילוּ פַּעַם אֶחָת -
הַלַּיְלָה הַזֶּה שְׁתֵּי פְעָמִים.
שֶׁבְּכָל הַלֵּילוֹת אָנוּ אוֹכְלִין בֵּין יוֹשְׁבִין וּבֵין מְסֻבִּין -
הַלַּיְלָה הַזֶּה כֻּלָּנוּ מְסֻבִּין.

What differentiates this night from all other nights?
On all other nights we eat chametz and matzah; tonight, only matzah.
On all other nights we eat a variety of vegetables; tonight, marror.
On all other nights, we don't dip our food, even one time;
  tonight [we dip] twice.
On all other nights, we eat either sitting or reclining; tonight we all recline.

Questions For Google

What does it mean and why does it matter?
How do I get there from here?
Where is the line that cannot be crossed?
Why is the first time the best?
Who will be coming and when will they get here?
How long will it last before it is over?
Who has the right and why do they have it?
Who is the most important one?
What did it mean and why did it matter?
If all is lost, how will I find it?
If not now, then when?
Are you real? Do you even exist?

—Elizabeth Spiers

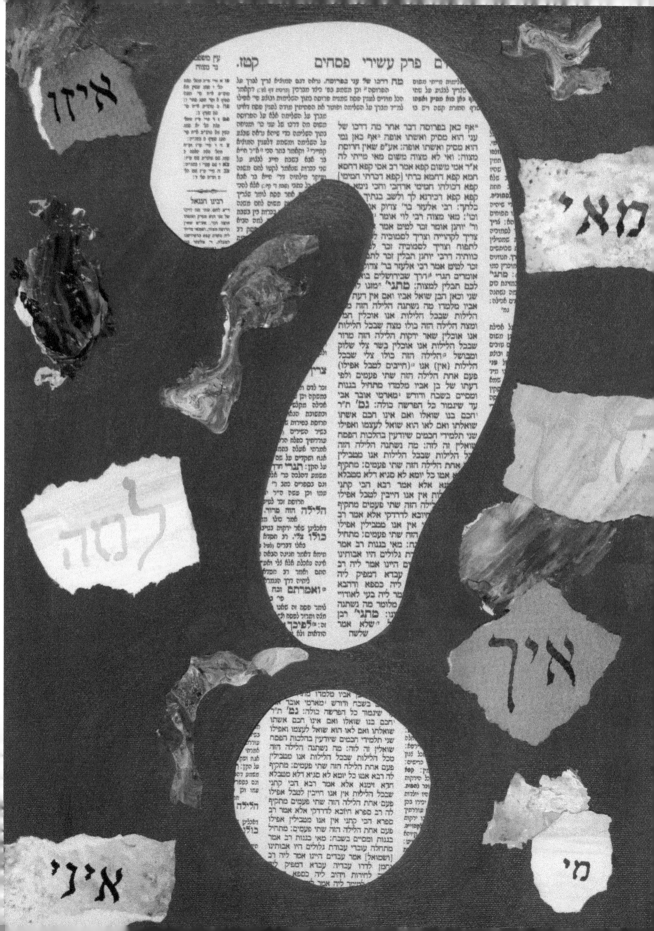

Beginning the Story, Shmuel Style

Our story starts with slavery in Egypt, following the talmudic sage Shmuel's opinion of where to begin (see left). We start with a summary of the major points of the story, followed by commentary and stories on the importance of the act of storytelling.

We were slaves to Pharaoh in the land of Egypt. And the Lord, our God, took us out from there with a strong hand and an outstretched forearm. And if the Holy Blessed One had not taken our ancestors from Egypt, we and our children and our children's children would all still be enslaved to Pharaoh in Egypt.

עֲבָדִים הָיִינוּ לְפַרְעֹה בְּמִצְרַיִם,
וַיּוֹצִיאֵנוּ יהוה אֱלֹהֵינוּ מִשָּׁם בְּיָד
חֲזָקָה וּבִזְרֹעַ נְטוּיָה. וְאִלּוּ לֹא
הוֹצִיא הַקָּדוֹשׁ בָּרוּךְ הוּא אֶת
אֲבוֹתֵינוּ מִמִּצְרַיִם, הֲרֵי אָנוּ וּבָנֵינוּ
וּבְנֵי בָנֵינוּ מְשֻׁעְבָּדִים הָיִינוּ לְפַרְעֹה
בְּמִצְרַיִם.

What Is Our Legacy?

"If God had not taken us from Egypt, we would still be stuck there—and our children and grandchildren too."

Ancient Egypt was a distant memory when this passage was written in the Geonic period (650–1075 CE). What does this passage mean, then?

What choices that we make today will last beyond our lifetimes? What will remain for a few generations? What will remain one or two thousand years from now?

We still remember the slavery and cruelty we experienced in Egypt. "Embrace the stranger for you, too, were a stranger in Egypt" remains an important principle of Jewish ethics.

What will future generations remember of our labor practices? Will we be an example of what to do or what not to do? What is our legacy?

While Ancient Egypt was long gone, the pyramids remained. They remain to this day. Which of our infrastructure, land use, environmental choices will last?

Carbon dioxide emitted today will stay in the atmosphere for 300 to 1000 years. What is our legacy?

Maggid: Avadim Hayinu   12

Start With Shame And End With Praise

The Talmud (Pesachim 116a) teaches:

מַתְחִיל בִּגְנוּת וּמְסַיֵּים בְּשֶׁבַח

[When telling the Passover story,] begin with shame and conclude with praise.

What do you think of this storytelling philosophy? Does it make sense with this story? What about as a theological statement? Rev. Dr. Martin Luther King Jr. famously said, "the arc of the moral universe is long, but it bends towards justice." Do you agree?

The Talmud continues:

מַאי בִּגְנוּת? רַב אָמַר: "מִתְּחִלָּה עוֹבְדֵי עֲבוֹדָה זָרָה הָיוּ אֲבוֹתֵינוּ". [וּשְׁמוּאֵל] אָמַר: "עֲבָדִים הָיִינוּ"

What is "with shame"? Rav says, "At the beginning our ancestors worshipped false idols." [Shmuel] says, "We were enslaved."

What are the implications of thinking that our origins as idol worshipers versus as slaves are shameful? What are the stories we tell about our ancestors? In the United States today, some of us have ancestors who were enslaved, while other ancestors worshipped the false idol of white supremacy. Which family stories are a source of shame and which are a source of strength?

The Talmud does not continue the discussion. Today, we ask:

מַאי בְּשֶׁבַח?

What is "in praise"?

Where do we end our stories? Do they end in gratitude? In praise? Is being able to tell our stories—potentially all night long as Rabbi Eliezer, Rabbi Yehoshua, Rabbi Elazar ben Azaria, Rabbi Akiva, and Rabbi Tarfon did—itself a happy ending? What does a "happy ending" mean to you?

Chag HaAviv
Environmental

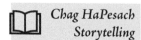
Chag HaPesach
Storytelling

Chag HaCheirut
Liberation

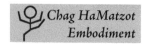
Chag HaMatzot
Embodiment

And even if we were all people full of wisdom, all people full of discernment, all elders, all knowledgeable about the Torah, we would still be commanded to tell the story of the Exodus from Egypt. And anyone who adds and spends extra time telling the story of the Exodus from Egypt, behold that is praiseworthy.

וַאֲפִילוּ כֻּלָּנוּ חֲכָמִים, כֻּלָּנוּ נְבוֹנִים, כֻּלָּנוּ זְקֵנִים, כֻּלָּנוּ יוֹדְעִים אֶת הַתּוֹרָה מִצְוָה עָלֵינוּ לְסַפֵּר בִּיצִיאַת מִצְרָיִם. וְכָל הַמַּרְבֶּה לְסַפֵּר בִּיצִיאַת מִצְרַיִם הֲרֵי זֶה מְשֻׁבָּח.

Even If We Were...

...all people full of wisdom   כֻּלָּנוּ חֲכָמִים
...all people full of discernment   כֻּלָּנוּ נְבוֹנִים
...all elders   כֻּלָּנוּ זְקֵנִים
...all knowledgeable about the Torah   כֻּלָּנוּ יוֹדְעִים אֶת הַתּוֹרָה

What are the differences in these categories?
Why does the text choose these categories as the paradigms of people who might not think they have to tell the story of the Exodus from Egypt yet another year?

One time Rabbi Eliezer, Rabbi Yehoshua, Rabbi Elazar ben Azariah, Rabbi Akiva, and Rabbi Tarfon were reclining in Bnei Brak and were telling the story of the Exodus from Egypt that whole night, until their students came and said to them, "The time for the morning Shema has arrived."

מַעֲשֶׂה בְּרַבִּי אֱלִיעֶזֶר וְרַבִּי יְהוֹשֻׁעַ וְרַבִּי אֶלְעָזָר בֶּן־עֲזַרְיָה וְרַבִּי עֲקִיבָא וְרַבִּי טַרְפוֹן שֶׁהָיוּ מְסֻבִּין בִּבְנֵי־בְרַק וְהָיוּ מְסַפְּרִים בִּיצִיאַת מִצְרַיִם כָּל־אוֹתוֹ הַלַּיְלָה, עַד שֶׁבָּאוּ תַלְמִידֵיהֶם וְאָמְרוּ לָהֶם רַבּוֹתֵינוּ הִגִּיעַ זְמַן קְרִיאַת שְׁמַע שֶׁל שַׁחֲרִית.

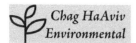
Chag HaAviv
Environmental

Chag HaPesach
Storytelling

Chag HaCheirut
Liberation

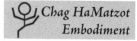
Chag HaMatzot
Embodiment

Rabbi Elazar ben Azariah said, "Look, I am like seventy years old and I have not merited [to understand why] the Exodus from Egypt should be said at night until Ben Zoma explained it, as it is stated (Deuteronomy 16:3), 'In order that you remember the day of your going out from the land of Egypt *all* the days of your life.'

'The days of your life' refers to the days. 'All the days of your life' refers to the nights. But the Sages say, "'the days of your life' refers to this world, 'all the days of your life' refers to the days of the Messiah."

אָמַר רַבִּי אֶלְעָזָר בֶּן־עֲזַרְיָה הֲרֵי אֲנִי כְּבֶן שִׁבְעִים שָׁנָה וְלֹא זָכִיתִי שֶׁתֵּאָמֵר יְצִיאַת מִצְרַיִם בַּלֵּילוֹת עַד שֶׁדְּרָשָׁה בֶּן זוֹמָא, שֶׁנֶּאֱמַר, לְמַעַן תִּזְכֹּר אֶת יוֹם צֵאתְךָ מֵאֶרֶץ מִצְרַיִם כֹּל יְמֵי חַיֶּיךָ.

יְמֵי חַיֶּיךָ הַיָּמִים. כֹּל יְמֵי חַיֶּיךָ הַלֵּילוֹת. וַחֲכָמִים אוֹמְרִים יְמֵי חַיֶּיךָ הָעוֹלָם הַזֶּה. כֹּל יְמֵי חַיֶּיךָ לְהָבִיא לִימוֹת הַמָּשִׁיחַ:

You're Aging Well

Why is it that as we grow older and stronger
The road signs point us adrift and make us afraid
Saying "You never can win," "Watch your back," "Where's your husband?"
Oh, I don't like the signs that the sign makers made.
So I'm going to steal out with my paint and brushes
I'll change the directions, I'll hit every street
It's the Tinseltown scandal, the Robin Hood vandal
She goes out and steals the king's English
And in the morning you wake up and the signs point to you
They say
"I'm so glad that you finally made it here,"
"You thought nobody cared, but I did, I could tell,"
And "This is your year, " and "It always starts here,"
And oh "You're aging well."

—Dar Williams (excerpt)

בָּרוּךְ הַמָּקוֹם, בָּרוּךְ הוּא, בָּרוּךְ שֶׁנָתַן תּוֹרָה לְ[עַמּוֹ] יִשְׂרָאֵל, בָּרוּךְ הוּא.

Blessed be the Place, Blessed be God; Blessed be the One who Gave the Torah to the people Israel, Blessed be God.

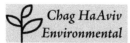
Chag HaAviv
Environmental

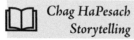
Chag HaPesach
Storytelling

Chag HaCheirut
Liberation

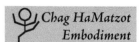
Chag HaMatzot
Embodiment

Four Children

How do we tell our stories and our traditions? How does it vary by who is listening?

"Box? What box? I don't see a box."

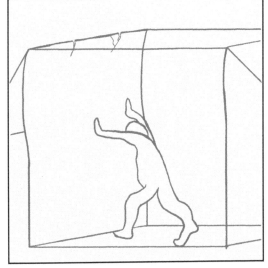

"If I just keep pushing, maybe I can break out of here"

What About The Child Who Is Not At The Table?

Like many of the sets of four in the Haggadah, there is a hidden fifth—the child who does not attend the seder at all. This Haggadah aims to bring in voices that are frequently silenced or ignored, but our communities and traditions can be alienating for many. While this Haggadah translates the "arba banim" as the "four children" and uses the singular they to refer to each of them, the literal translation is "four sons" and the Hebrew uses male pronouns.

Whose voices are missing from our texts? stories? tables?

The Torah speaks about four children: one is wise, one is wicked, one is innocent, and one does not know how to ask questions.

כְּנֶגֶד אַרְבָּעָה בָנִים דִּבְּרָה תוֹרָה:
אֶחָד חָכָם,
וְאֶחָד רָשָׁע,
וְאֶחָד תָּם,
וְאֶחָד שֶׁאֵינוֹ יוֹדֵעַ לִשְׁאוֹל.

"Here we are. Green baby goes in the green box."

"These boxes are evil and must be destroyed, no matter the cost."

The four children in the art are unlabeled. Which child is which?
Can you make arguments from multiple angles?

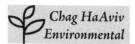 Chag HaAviv
Environmental

 Chag HaPesach
Storytelling

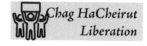 Chag HaCheirut
Liberation

 Chag HaMatzot
Embodiment

חָכָם מָה הוּא אוֹמֵר? מָה הָעֵדֹת וְהַחֻקִּים וְהַמִּשְׁפָּטִים אֲשֶׁר צִוָּה יהוה אֱלֹהֵינוּ אֶתְכֶם? וְאַף אַתָּה אֱמוֹר לוֹ כְּהִלְכוֹת הַפֶּסַח: אֵין מַפְטִירִין אַחַר הַפֶּסַח אֲפִיקוֹמָן:

What does the wise child say? "'What are the testimonies, statutes, and judgments that the Lord our God commanded you?' (Deuteronomy 6:20)" And accordingly you will say to them, as per the laws of the Pesach sacrifice, "We may not eat an afikoman [a dessert or other foods eaten after the meal] after [we are finished eating] the Pesach sacrifice (Mishnah Pesachim 10:8)."

Sources On Wisdom

אֵיזֶהוּ חָכָם? הַלּוֹמֵד מִכָּל אָדָם.
Who is wise? One who learns from everyone. (Pirkei Avot 4:1)

מָה־רַבּוּ מַעֲשֶׂיךָ יהוה כֻּלָּם בְּחָכְמָה עָשִׂיתָ מָלְאָה הָאָרֶץ קִנְיָנֶךָ.
How diverse is your creation, God; you made them all in wisdom and filled the earth with your creation. (Psalms 104:24)

כִּי בְּרֹב חָכְמָה רָב־כָּעַס.
For as wisdom grows, frustration grows. (Kohelet 1:18)

The Policy Wonk

The wise child is focused on the highly specific legislative details. How many of us have been excited about environmental legislation, only to discover that it provides loopholes that set us back? Or that a bill we thought was unambiguously harmful actually contains important steps forward?

The wise child understands that in Judaism and in policy, the real work happens in the details of the interpretative process.

Modes of Learning

We jump right to the details of the meal with the wise child. It seems like an odd response, since the wise child asks about "testimonies, statutes, and judgments." This person needs to be reminded that Pesach is not wholly cerebral. The seder is an embodied experience. The academically inclined student needs to be reminded of their body and other ways of knowing and learning.

Wisdom in Ritual And Law

Jewish tradition emphasizes ritual, obligation, and law; an emphasis decidedly countercultural to many of the secular societies Jews live in.

What wisdom do you find in Jewish ritual and law? Do you lean into or away from obligation and commandment? Why?

רָשָׁע מָה הוּא אוֹמֵר? מָה הָעֲבוֹדָה הַזֹּאת לָכֶם? לָכֶם - וְלֹא לוֹ. וּלְפִי שֶׁהוֹצִיא אֶת עַצְמוֹ מִן הַכְּלָל כָּפַר בְּעִקָּר. וְאַף אַתָּה הַקְהֵה אֶת שִׁנָּיו וֶאֱמוֹר לוֹ: "בַּעֲבוּר זֶה עָשָׂה יהוה לִי בְּצֵאתִי מִמִּצְרָיִם". לִי וְלֹא־לוֹ. אִלּוּ הָיָה שָׁם, לֹא הָיָה נִגְאָל:

What does the evil child say? "'What is this worship to you?' (Exodus 12:26)" "To you' and not 'to them.' They excluded themselves from the community, so they remain apart. Accordingly, you will blunt their teeth and say to them, "'For the sake of this, God did this for me in my going out of Egypt' (Exodus 13:8)." "For me' and not 'for them.' If they had been there, they would not have been saved.

A Happier Ending

Is the question the "wicked" child asks really so bad? "What does this mean to you" can be a respectful and kind question.

Since we only have a written tradition here, we have to fill in the tone of voice ourselves. Sometimes, "this child has excluded themselves from the community" becomes a self-fulfilling prophecy. Are there better ways to tell this story that could result in a happier ending?

Invasive Species

Theoretically, invasive species are plants or animals that come from an external habitat and cause harm in their new home. However, scientists debate these labels. How should we define what is "native" or "external," especially given climate change? How do we define "harm"? Some species are endangered in their native habitat, but invasive elsewhere.

When does it make sense to label something as harmful, and when does the label itself do more harm?

A Violent Response

The response to the wicked child is a physical response. The Hebrew can be translated as "you will blunt their teeth" or even "you will punch their teeth." Is this type of response ever appropriate in an educational or communal context? When is violence justified, if ever?

Boundaries And Limits

Where are the boundaries on your community? What does it take for someone to exclude themselves from the community?

Do you think your circles are too quick or too slow to push out people who are beyond the line? What harm occurs in each scenario?

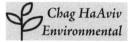 *Chag HaAviv* **Environmental**

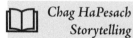 *Chag HaPesach* **Storytelling**

 *Chag HaCheirut* **Liberation**

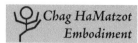 *Chag HaMatzot* **Embodiment**

תָּם מָה הוּא אוֹמֵר? מַה זֹּאת?
וְאָמַרְתָּ אֵלָיו "בְּחֹזֶק יָד הוֹצִיאָנוּ יהוה מִמִּצְרַיִם מִבֵּית עֲבָדִים".

What does the innocent/simple/wholehearted child say? "'What is this?' (Exodus 13:14)" And you will say to them, "'God used God's strong hand to take us out from Egypt, from the house of slaves' (Exodus 13:14)."

Embodiment

Jacob is famously described as tam: in comparison to his twin Esav, who is a hunter and "a man of the fields," Jacob is tam and dwells in tents (Genesis 25:27).

The text indicates the opposite of "tam" is "outdoorsman." Does that resonate with your vision of embodiment?

Think about Jacob's life, including his deception of his father, time with Laban, and physical encounter with the angel. Does he seem like a tam? Why does the text describe him that way?

Wholeness In Complexity

Nature is gloriously messy. Evolution is the result of random mutations at a cellular level. God's world is full of diversity and complexity.

The word tam reflects wholeness as well as simplicity. Do you see the tam in the wholeness and complexity of the natural world, looking at the whole story with all of its contradictions? Or does the tam create false simplicity and sterilized monocultures?

The Essence

The wholehearted child's question "what is this" gets to the essence of the seder. God freed us from slavery... so we celebrate this holiday every year. So we recognize oppression and value liberation. So we make sure to support the refugee and the needy today.

When do simple questions lead us to profound truths, and when do they gloss over important complexity?

Unquestioning Faith Is Not A Virtue

An activist's faith can never be unquestioning, can never stop responding to "new passions and new forces," can never oversimplify, as believers and activists are often tempted or pressured to do.
—Adrienne Rich, *What is Found There*

וְשֶׁאֵינוֹ יוֹדֵעַ לִשְׁאוֹל – אַתְּ פְּתַח לוֹ, שֶׁנֶּאֱמַר, וְהִגַּדְתָּ לְבִנְךָ בַּיּוֹם הַהוּא לֵאמֹר, בַּעֲבוּר זֶה עָשָׂה יהוה לִי בְּצֵאתִי מִמִּצְרָיִם.

And the one who doesn't know to ask, you will open the conversation for them. As it is stated (Exodus 13:8), "And you will speak to your child on that day saying, 'for the sake of this God did this for me when I was leaving Egypt.'"

Moses, Too, Struggled With Speech

וַיֹּאמֶר מֹשֶׁה אֶל־יהוה בִּי אֲדֹנָי לֹא אִישׁ דְּבָרִים אָנֹכִי גַּם מִתְּמוֹל גַּם מִשִּׁלְשֹׁם גַּם מֵאָז דַּבֶּרְךָ אֶל־עַבְדֶּךָ כִּי כְבַד־פֶּה וּכְבַד לָשׁוֹן אָנֹכִי:

But Moses said to God, "Please, my Lord, I have never been a man of words, either in times past or now that You have spoken to Your servant; I am heavy of speech and heavy of tongue." (Exodus 4:10)

A Silent, Connected Web

The trees revealed startling secrets. I discovered that they are in a web of interdependence, linked by a system of underground channels, where they perceive and connect and relate... The old and the young [trees] are perceiving, communicating, and responding to each other by emitting chemical signals. Chemicals identical to our own neurotransmitters. Signals created by ions cascading across fungal membranes.
—Suzanne Simard, *Finding the Mother Tree*

Cannot or Does Not Ask

The Torah quote for this child is identical to the one given for the wicked child. The rabbis provided several possibilities why: Maybe the differences in the parent's tone are so significant that the responses are not the same at all.

Perhaps this child is most likely to be influenced by the wicked child.

Or maybe they can ask, but choose not to, disengaging from the seder like their sibling.

Open the Conversation

"You will open the conversation for them." This teaches that providing ways for children to communicate is an affirmative obligation for parents and teachers. This applies to all kinds of assistive technology and sign language. All Jewish children should have ways to communicate their needs and ask questions about our heritage.

 *Chag HaAviv* Environmental

 *Chag HaPesach* Storytelling

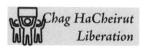 *Chag HaCheirut* Liberation

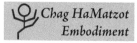 *Chag HaMatzot* Embodiment

The Vernal Equinox

Passover starts on the 15th of Nissan, which is the first full moon following the vernal equinox. When we sit down to the seder—anywhere in the world—the amount of daylight and nighttime is just about equal. In the Northern hemisphere, the days start getting longer following Passover.

What is the relationship between the equinox and the themes of Passover?

Are We Late To Start the Storytelling Now?

The Haggadah now asks if we should have started telling the Exodus story two weeks ago on Rosh Chodesh. The answer plays off the text from the evil child and the child who does not know how to ask:

וְהִגַּדְתָּ לְבִנְךָ בַּיּוֹם הַהוּא לֵאמֹר בַּעֲבוּר זֶה עָשָׂה יהוה לִי בְּצֵאתִי מִמִּצְרָיִם.

And you will speak to your child on that day saying "for the sake of this, God did this for me when I was leaving Egypt." (Exodus 13:8).

The Haggadah uses the odd phrasing of "on that day" and "for the sake of this" to explain why we are right on time with the Seder.

Could it be that we should be discussing the Exodus starting on Rosh Chodesh? That is why the Torah says "on that day" (Exodus 13:8).

But when it says "on that day," could it mean during daylight? That is why the text says "for the sake of this." For the sake of what? For the sake of the Pesach seder, that is, at the time when the matzah and maror are on the table in front of you.

יָכוֹל מֵרֹאשׁ חֹדֶשׁ? תַּלְמוּד לוֹמַר בַּיּוֹם הַהוּא.
אִי בַּיּוֹם הַהוּא יָכוֹל מִבְּעוֹד יוֹם? תַּלְמוּד לוֹמַר בַּעֲבוּר זֶה – בַּעֲבוּר זֶה לֹא אָמַרְתִּי, אֶלָּא בְּשָׁעָה שֶׁיֵּשׁ מַצָּה וּמָרוֹר מֻנָּחִים לְפָנֶיךָ.

Time Passes

Time too is afraid of passing, is riddled with holes
through which time feels itself leaking.
Time sweats in the middle of the night
when all the other dimensions are sleeping.
Time has lost every picture of itself as a child.
Now time is old, leathery and slow.
Can't sneak up on anyone anymore,
Can't hide in the grass, can't run, can't catch.
Can't figure out how not to trample
what it means to bless.

—Joy Ladin

25

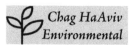
Chag HaAviv
Environmental

Chag HaPesach
Storytelling

Chag HaCheirut
Liberation

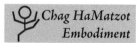
Chag HaMatzot
Embodiment

Beginning the Story, Rav Style

Our story re-starts with our ancestors' spiritual journey, following the talmudic sage Rav's opinion of where to begin (see page 12). This version starts with idolatry, includes Esav's inheritance, and emphasizes God's covenantal relationship with the Jewish people.

From the beginning, our ancestors were idol worshipers. And now, the Place [of all] has brought us close to work together in worship as it is stated (Joshua 24:2-4), "Yehoshua said to the whole people, so said the Lord, God of Israel, 'Your ancestors historically lived over the river— Terach the father of Abraham and the father of Nachor, and they worshiped other gods.

מִתְּחִלָּה עוֹבְדֵי עֲבוֹדָה זָרָה הָיוּ אֲבוֹתֵינוּ, וְעַכְשָׁיו קֵרְבָנוּ הַמָּקוֹם לַעֲבֹדָתוֹ, שֶׁנֶּאֱמַר: וַיֹּאמֶר יְהוֹשֻׁעַ אֶל־כָּל־הָעָם, כֹּה אָמַר יהוה אֱלֹהֵי יִשְׂרָאֵל: בְּעֵבֶר הַנָּהָר יָשְׁבוּ אֲבוֹתֵיכֶם מֵעוֹלָם, תֶּרַח אֲבִי אַבְרָהָם וַאֲבִי נָחוֹר, וַיַּעַבְדוּ אֱלֹהִים אֲחֵרִים.

The Past Is Always Working On Us And Through Us

We so often think of the past as something like a nature reserve: a discrete, bounded place we can visit in our imaginations to make us feel better. I wonder how we could learn to recognize that the past is always working on us and through us, and that diversity, in all its forms, human and natural, is strength. That messy stretches of species-rich vegetation with all their attendant invertebrate life are better, just *better*, than the eerie, impoverished silence of modern planting schemes and fields. I wonder how we might learn to align our aesthetic and moral landscapes to fit that intuition. I wonder. I think of the meadow. Those clouds of butterflies have met with local extinction, but held in that soil is a bank of seeds that will hang on.

—Helen Macdonald, *Vesper Flights*

"'And I took your father, Abraham, from over the river and I walked him through all the land of Canaan and I increased his seed and I gave him Isaac. And I gave to Isaac, Jacob and Esav; and I gave to Esav, Mount Seir to inherit it; and Yaakov and his household went down to Egypt.'"

וָאֶקַּח אֶת־אֲבִיכֶם אֶת־אַבְרָהָם מֵעֵבֶר הַנָּהָר וָאוֹלֵךְ אוֹתוֹ בְּכָל־אֶרֶץ כְּנַעַן, וָאַרְבֶּה אֶת־זַרְעוֹ וָאֶתֶּן לוֹ אֶת־יִצְחָק, וָאֶתֵּן לְיִצְחָק אֶת־יַעֲקֹב וְאֶת־עֵשָׂו. וָאֶתֵּן לְעֵשָׂו אֶת־הַר שֵׂעִיר לָרֶשֶׁת אֹתוֹ, וְיַעֲקֹב וּבָנָיו יָרְדוּ מִצְרָיִם.

Universalism or Particularism

Why does the Haggadah mention Esav here? What is it trying to teach us about how God relates to our neighbors and to all of humanity?

Mountain of Demons

Many commentators reject a universalist message here. Instead, they call Mount Seir the "Mountain of Demons"* and highlight Esav's short-sightedness and physicality.
   Our traditions includes a rich diversity of voices. Some may resonate strongly, and some may feel foreign and even distasteful. How do we hold all aspects of our tradition, while still making meaning for ourselves today?

*This interpretation relies on Isaiah 13:21, which uses the word "seirim" (related to Mount Seir) to mean a satyr or demon.

"I Walked Him Through"

This text goes out of its way to describe how God made Abraham walk through the whole land of Canaan. In contrast, Esav is given Mount Seir to inherit with no further action.
   How does the physical act of walking the land change your relationship to it?

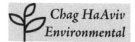 Chag HaAviv
Environmental

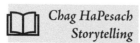 Chag HaPesach
Storytelling

 Chag HaCheirut
Liberation

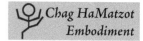 Chag HaMatzot
Embodiment

Blessed be the One who keeps promises to Israel, blessed be God; since the Holy Blessed One foresaw the endgame. God said to Abraham, our father, in the Covenant between the Pieces, as it is stated (Genesis 15:13-14), "[And God said to Avram,] 'you should surely know that your seed will be a stranger in a land that is not theirs, and they will enslave them and afflict them four hundred years. And also I will judge that nation for which they shall toil, and afterwards they will go out with much property.'"

בָּרוּךְ שׁוֹמֵר הַבְטָחָתוֹ לְיִשְׂרָאֵל, בָּרוּךְ הוּא. שֶׁהַקָּדוֹשׁ בָּרוּךְ הוּא חִשַּׁב אֶת־הַקֵּץ, לַעֲשׂוֹת כְּמוֹ שֶׁאָמַר לְאַבְרָהָם אָבִינוּ בִּבְרִית בֵּין הַבְּתָרִים, שֶׁנֶּאֱמַר: יָדֹעַ תֵּדַע כִּי־גֵר יִהְיֶה זַרְעֲךָ בְּאֶרֶץ לֹא לָהֶם, וַעֲבָדוּם וְעִנּוּ אֹתָם אַרְבַּע מֵאוֹת שָׁנָה. וְגַם אֶת־הַגּוֹי אֲשֶׁר יַעֲבֹדוּ דָן אָנֹכִי וְאַחֲרֵי־כֵן יֵצְאוּ בִּרְכֻשׁ גָּדוֹל.

Reparations

Reparations were part of the Torah's vision of slavery and freedom, from the time of Abraham. The rabbis of the Talmud (BT Sanhedrin 91a) pick up on this theme. They envision the Egyptians bringing Jews to court, saying, "you stole our gold and silver when you left Egypt! We never intended that you take it forever, and we want it back." According to the story, Geviha argues on behalf of the Jewish community:

[Geviha] asked, "From where are you bringing your proof?"
They said, "From the Torah."
He said, "So I will also use the Torah as proof, as it says, 'And the length of time that Bnei Yisrael dwelt in Egypt was 430 years' (Exodus 12:40). Give us backpay for 600,000 workers for 430 years!"

אמר להן "מהיכן אתם מביאין ראייה?"
אמרו לו "מן התורה."
אמר להן "אף אני לא אביא לכם ראייה אלא מן התורה, שנאמר ומושב בני ישראל אשר ישבו במצרים שלשים שנה וארבע מאות שנה. תנו לנו שכר עבודה של ששים ריבוא ששיעבדתם במצרים שלשים שנה וארבע מאות שנה!"

The Egyptians in the story cannot respond to this claim and run away, leaving sown fields and planted vineyards behind.
How do the reparations change the story of slavery in Egypt?
How does the promise of reparations change
the covenant between God and Abraham?
How does this part of our tradition impact the way we envision justice today?

Resilience In Jewish History

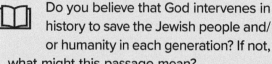

Do you believe that God intervenes in history to save the Jewish people and/or humanity in each generation? If not, what might this passage mean?

The Ephod Bad Haggadah commentary (Rabbi Benjamin David Rabinowitz, Warsaw, 1872) writes that the telling of the Exodus story itself saves Jews in each generation. Similarly, Ahad Ha'am (poet, 1856–1927) famously said "More than Jews have kept Shabbat, Shabbat has kept the Jews."

Do you agree with them? Are there other aspects of Jewish religious practice, cultural heritage, or communal stories that you think have been protective or built Jewish resilience across generations?

Covenantal Partners

The Torah is full of commitments between God and humanity and between God and the Jewish people: the covenant with Noah and the rainbow; covenants with each Abraham, Isaac, and Jacob; Mount Sinai; the blessings and curses in the desert; and others.

What commitments between God and the Jewish people or between God and humanity speak to you? Have we lived up to our end of those commitments? How can we be God's partners in ending oppression and building a better world?

Resilience at a Cellular Level

Spring peepers, a chorus frog native to eastern North America, typically come out of hibernation around the same time as Passover. They spend the winter in frozen ponds or under logs. Unlike most other amphibians, these frogs can survive freezing. Their cells expel their water so ice crystals do not damage the organelles in the cells. The concentrated sugars in the cells make a natural antifreeze. The frogs can survive in cold as low as 20 degrees Farenheit.

What kinds of resilience are found in your body? What kinds of resilience do you aspire to?

Trauma Can Build On Itself

After a wildfire, all rain can cause major flash flooding. The fire destroys the roots that hold the soil in place, and change the electrical charge of the soil so it repels water. Suddenly, a small rainshower can cause major floods. It takes two to five years to return to normal.

Sometimes adversity builds strength and resilience. Other times, trauma builds on itself, leaving a person or community more vulnerable. Healing can be elusive and slow.

What model of healing speaks to you? What role do God's commitments play?

Cover the matzah and lift your glass.

וְהִיא שֶׁעָמְדָה לַאֲבוֹתֵינוּ וְלָנוּ. שֶׁלֹּא אֶחָד בִּלְבָד עָמַד עָלֵינוּ לְכַלּוֹתֵנוּ, אֶלָּא שֶׁבְּכָל דּוֹר וָדוֹר עוֹמְדִים עָלֵינוּ לְכַלּוֹתֵנוּ, וְהַקָּדוֹשׁ בָּרוּךְ הוּא מַצִּילֵנוּ מִיָּדָם.

And it is this [commitment] that has stood for our ancestors and for us. It is not only one historical person or nation that has tried to destroy us, but rather a pattern in each generation. They stand against us to destroy us, but the Holy Blessed One rescues us from their hand.

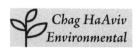 *Chag HaAviv* **Environmental**

 *Chag HaPesach* **Storytelling**

 *Chag HaCheirut* **Liberation**

Chag HaMatzot **Embodiment**

Stories Within Stories: A Close Read

We come back to the Exodus story through a retelling from Deuteronomy. Each verse and each phrase is elucidated through rabbinic stories.

Go out and learn (Deuteronomy 26:5), *"Arami oved avi.* Then my father went down to Egypt, and resided there with a small number and he became there a nation, great, powerful and numerous."

צֵא וּלְמַד: אֲרַמִּי אֹבֵד אָבִי, וַיֵּרֶד מִצְרַיְמָה וַיָּגָר שָׁם בִּמְתֵי מְעָט, וַיְהִי שָׁם לְגוֹי גָּדוֹל, עָצוּם וָרָב.

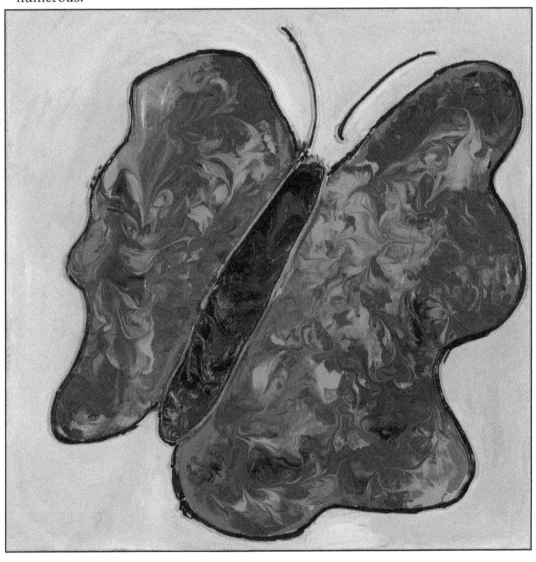

Arami Oved Avi

Arami means an Aramean. But who?
Oved means either "oppressed" or "wandering."
Avi means my father. But which one?

One traditional reading is "an Aramean oppressed my father." The Haggadah often introduces this portion as "Go out and learn what Lavan the Aramean did to my father. Pharaoh decreed against only the males, but Lavan sought to uproot the whole."

How does the story change when it starts with fighting within a family? With persecution?

Another option is to read *oved* as an adjective: "my father was a wandering Aramean." This may refer to Jacob, who lived in Aram with Lavan. Sforno (c. 1470–1550, Italy) read the text this way, and added that Jacob was effectively homeless while he was living in Aram, and did not have the stability to raise his family to become a nation.

What does it mean for us that our story couldn't begin until after our ancestors had found stable housing?

Rashbam (c. 1085–1174, France) understood the statement to be about Abraham rather than Jacob as in "my father Abraham was a wandering Aramean." Abraham left Aram when God told him to go to a new land.

History is full of immigration. Sometimes people leave in search for better opportunities or religious freedom. Other times people leave as refugees.

What does immigration feel like in our bodies? Is all immigration "wandering"? What does it mean to wander?

Monarch butterflies migrate from Canada to Mexico, a journey of up to 2,500 miles. The butterflies travel as individuals and in groups. The migration takes multiple generations of butterflies. Somehow the butterflies born in Canada know to fly south to the same exact Mexican forests their ancestors left.

What kinds of migration, wandering and/or persecutions feel cyclical to you? What ancestral paths do you follow?

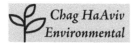 *Chag HaAviv* Environmental

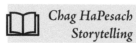 *Chag HaPesach* Storytelling

 *Chag HaCheirut* Liberation

 *Chag HaMatzot* Embodiment

Strangers In A Strange Land

Jews have been wandering since Biblical times. We have rarely felt truly at home and have often left in haste, as refugees. These stories are often complex and multi-layered, and can be radically different depending on who is telling the story. Consider these two descendents of Sefardi Jews whose families were forcibly exiled from Spain in 1492.

Jose M. Estrugo was a Sephardic Jew born in the Ottoman empire. He immigrated to America in his youth and became a founding member of the Sephardic community of Los Angeles. In 1922, he visited Spain. A decade later, he wrote about his trip:

"For the first time in my life, I felt truly aboriginal, native. Here I was not, I could not be an intruder! For the first time, I felt very much at home, much more so than in the Jewish quarter where I was born! I am not ashamed to confess that I bent down, in an outburst of indescribable emotion, and kissed the ground upon which I tread for the first time, nearly a century after the end of the Inquisition."
(translation from Ladino by Aviva Ben Ur)

Emma Lazarus was a Sefardic Jew born in New York City. Her family were among the first Jews in New Amsterdam, fleeing the inquisition in Recife, Brazil. She wrote a poem about 1492:

Thou two-faced year, Mother of Change and Fate,
Didst weep when Spain cast forth with flaming
 sword,
The children of the prophets of the Lord,
Prince, priest, and people, spurned by zealot hate.
Hounded from sea to sea, from state to state,
The West refused them, and the East abhorred.
No anchorage the known world could afford,
Close-locked was every port, barred every gate.
Then smiling, thou unveil'dst, O two-faced year,
A virgin world where doors of sunset part,
Saying, "Ho, all who weary, enter here!
There falls each ancient barrier that the art
Of race or creed or rank devised, to rear
Grim bulwarked hatred between heart and heart!"

How do these responses to a shared heritage contrast? What do they have in common? How do they each relate to the concept of homeland and indigeneity? How can we as Jews grapple with Emma Lazarus's vision of a "virgin world" that did serve as a refuge for many of our ancestors, when that vision relies on the genocide of the native peoples who lived here for thousands of years before 1492?

"And he went down to Egypt"—coerced by the Word [in which God told Abraham that his descendants would have to go into exile].

"And he resided there"—this teaches that Jacob, our father, didn't go down to settle in Egypt, but rather only to reside there, as it is stated (Genesis 47:4), "And they said to Pharaoh, 'To reside in the land have we come, since there is not enough pasture for your servant's flocks, since the famine is heavy in the land of Canaan, and now please grant that your servants should dwell in the Land of Goshen.'"

וַיֵּרֶד מִצְרַיְמָה – אָנוּס עַל פִּי הַדִּבּוּר.

וַיָּגָר שָׁם. מְלַמֵּד שֶׁלֹא יָרַד יַעֲקֹב אָבִינוּ לְהִשְׁתַּקֵּעַ בְּמִצְרַיִם אֶלָּא לָגוּר שָׁם, שֶׁנֶּאֱמַר: וַיֹּאמְרוּ אֶל־פַּרְעֹה, לָגוּר בָּאָרֶץ בָּאנוּ, כִּי אֵין מִרְעֶה לַצֹּאן אֲשֶׁר לַעֲבָדֶיךָ, כִּי כָבֵד הָרָעָב בְּאֶרֶץ כְּנָעַן. וְעַתָּה יֵשְׁבוּ־נָא עֲבָדֶיךָ בְּאֶרֶץ גֹּשֶׁן.

Forgotten Factors

The way the Haggadah tells the story, Jacob's life was planned and ordained before he was born. God told Abraham that his descendants would spend time as strangers in Egypt, therefore Abraham's descendents had no choice but to do so.

However, in the context of their lives, Jacob's family experienced another kind of constraint: they moved to Egypt because of a drought. They needed more water, so they moved away from reliance on rain and toward relying on the Nile.

How frequently are our decisions driven by environmental or other systemic factors that go unacknowledged when our stories are told?

 Chag HaAviv
Environmental

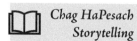 Chag HaPesach
Storytelling

 Chag HaCheirut
Liberation

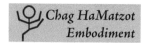 Chag HaMatzot
Embodiment

"As a small number"—as it is stated (Deuteronomy 10:22), "With seventy souls did your ancestors come down to Egypt, and now the Lord your God has made you as numerous as the stars of the sky."

"And he became there a nation"—[this] teaches that Israel [became] exceptional there.

בִּמְתֵי מְעָט. כְּמָה שֶׁנֶּאֱמַר: בְּשִׁבְעִים נֶפֶשׁ יָרְדוּ אֲבוֹתֶיךָ מִצְרָיְמָה, וְעַתָּה שָׂמְךָ יהוה אֱלֹהֶיךָ כְּכוֹכְבֵי הַשָּׁמַיִם לָרֹב. וַיְהִי שָׁם לְגוֹי. מְלַמֵּד שֶׁהָיוּ יִשְׂרָאֵל מְצֻיָּנִים שָׁם.

National Identity

One way to understand the word *"metzuyanim"* is as "becoming tziyon" (zion). Commentators have understood this process of becoming a great nation—growing from Jacob's familial clan into Bnei Yisrael, a nation and a people—in a variety of ways. Here are a few of the themes.

It is a question of strength and numbers.	*They stayed true to themselves and resisted assimilation.*	*It is about character and values.*
Midrash Tanchuma picks up on the animalistic language "and Bnei Yisrael spawned and swarmed." The midrash shares that each pregnancy among the Israelites yielded multiples:	Rabbi Yehudah Yudel Rosenberg (1860–1936, Poland and Canada) understands "metzuyanim" ("exceptional") to mean that the people stayed true to being Israelites and did not adopt Egyptian clothing or hairstyles.	Rabbi Baruch HaLevi Epstein (author of the Torah Temima, 1860–1942, Belarus) focuses on the word "gadol" ("great"), which can refer either to quantity or to quality. He writes that the matter of greatness here refers to how the people elevated honor (kavod) and glory
"Our sages said: They bore twins. Others say: Six were formed in a single womb. Others say: twelve were born from one womb. And still others contend six hundred thousand."	He explains, "anyone who saw them immediately knew they were Israelites; eventually they recognized "Israel," as a separate ethnic group. If they had become assimilated they would have been designated	(hiddur). He compares Bnei Yisrael in Egypt to the dove in Song of Songs. Just as the dove is special and the most humble of all the birds, so too did Bnei Yisrael distinguish themselves through elevating
Rabbi Yedidiah Tiah Weil (1721–1805, Central Europe) adds that the children were healthy and strong (as it says "great, powerful") and could walk immediately upon birth.	as Egyptians, God forbid, and they would not have been worthy of redemption."	Torah, even in Egypt, before revelation.
How does the size of a community impact your relationship to it?	*How does being separated impact identity and connection to a group?*	*Does this ring true to you about the Israelites in Egypt? How do different communities distinguish themselves today?*

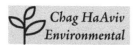
Chag HaAviv
Environmental

Chag HaPesach
Storytelling

Chag HaCheirut
Liberation

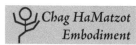
Chag HaMatzot
Embodiment

The Language of Those Who First Loved You

The language "spawned and swarmed and grew numerous" is dehumanizing. The word for spawned here, "vayishratzu," is related to the Hebrew word for "creepy crawly insect." In the Exodus text, it is simply presented as fact—the news, not a quote or the editorial page. It is an Egyptian point of view, of course, and a highly disrespectful and distancing one. How frequently do we internalize oppressive perspectives and adopt them as our own?

What do we remember and what do we forget? How do we name and categorize what we can barely observe, for what purpose, with what results. For example, there is only one marine mammal that the dominant scientific community calls by their Indigenous name...

Tuxuci, named in the Tupi language, has kept her name all through this colonization, while most other marine mammals are named after a colonizer at worst and hailed by a bland western description at best. It's a miracle. We say her name.

This is my prayer. May anyone who seeks to mention you be called to learn the language of those who first loved you. May you study the pink of yourself. Know yourself riverine and coast. May you taste the fresh and the saltwater of yourself and know what only you can know. May you live in the mouth of the river, meeting place of the tides, may all blessings flow through you.

I love you impossible dolphin, quietest in the river, breathing close to the surface. I'm grateful for what you remember even if you never say. And I'm keeping your name in my mouth like a river eternal, like this love ever flowing. I am keeping your name in my mouth, every day. All day.

—Alexis Pauline Gumbs, *Undrowned*

"Great, powerful"—as it is stated (Exodus 1:7), "And Bnei Yisrael spawned and swarmed and grew numerous and strong; very, very much so, and the land became full of them."

גָּדוֹל עָצוּם – כְּמָה שֶׁנֶּאֱמַר: וּבְנֵי יִשְׂרָאֵל פָּרוּ וַיִּשְׁרְצוּ וַיִּרְבּוּ וַיַּעַצְמוּ בִּמְאֹד מְאֹד, וַתִּמָּלֵא הָאָרֶץ אֹתָם.

Spawned and Swarmed and Grew Numerous

Consider the ordinary barnacle, the rock barnacle. Inside every one of those millions of hard white cones on the rocks—the kind that bruises your heel as you bruise its head—is of course a creature as alive as you or I...As it grows, it sheds its skin like lobster, enlarges its shell, and reproduces itself without end. The larvae "hatch into the sea in milky clouds." The barnacles encrusting a single half mile of shoreline can leak into the water a million million larvae. How many is that to a human mouthful?

...Sea water seems suddenly to be but a broth of barnacle bits. Can I fancy that a million million human infants are more real? ...I don't know if each barnacle larva is of itself unique and special, or if we the people are essentially as interchangeable as bricks. My brain is full of numbers; they swell and would split my skull like a shell. I examine the trapezoids of skin covering the back of my hands like blown dust motes moistened to clay. I have hatched, too, with millions of my kind, into a milky way that spreads from an unknown shore.

—Annie Dillard, *Pilgrim at Tinker Creek*

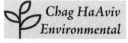 Chag HaAviv *Environmental*

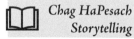 Chag HaPesach *Storytelling*

 Chag HaCheirut *Liberation*

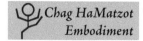 Chag HaMatzot *Embodiment*

If you are using a blood orange on your seder plate, point to it while reading this passage.

"And numerous" — as it is stated (Ezekiel 16:7, 6), "I let you grow like the plants of the field; and you continued to grow up until you attained to womanhood, until your breasts became firm and your hair sprouted. You were still naked and bare. And I passed by you and saw you lying in your blood, and I said to you 'live in your blood' and I said 'live in your blood.'"

וָרָב. כְּמָה שֶׁנֶּאֱמַר: רְבָבָה כְּצֶמַח הַשָּׂדֶה נְתַתִּיךְ, וַתִּרְבִּי וַתִּגְדְּלִי וַתָּבֹאִי בַּעֲדִי עֲדָיִים, שָׁדַיִם נָכֹנוּ וּשְׂעָרֵךְ צִמֵּחַ, וְאַתְּ עֵרֹם וְעֶרְיָה. וָאֶעֱבֹר עָלַיִךְ וָאֶרְאֵךְ מִתְבּוֹסֶסֶת בְּדָמָיִךְ, וָאֹמַר לָךְ בְּדָמַיִךְ חֲיִי, וָאֹמַר לָךְ בְּדָמַיִךְ חֲיִי.

Which Blood?

The Hagaddah reverses the order of the original text in Ezekiel. The original refers to a child, newly born and still bloody, abandoned in a field who then grows up like a weed. The Hagaddah's reversal changes the referant for the blood from the birthing blood to menstrual blood.

The Blood of the World

The Talmud Yerushalmi (Shabbat 2:6) teaches:

אדם הראשון דמו של עולם

The original Adam was the blood of the world.

What does it mean to be the blood of the world? What does it mean to live in or through your blood?

Tzipporah: Exodus 4:22-26

My father called me Tzipporah,
He knew that I would fly away.
Don't call me "little bird,"
Only an eagle rends flesh in flight.
The splash of blood on your doorstep
Is mine. Does it defile you
or protect you from the shadow
of death that steals
across Egypt's roads and pauses
at the threshold?
Is it the sea that splits for you
to walk across: safe,
To a fertile land?

—Alana Suskin (excerpt)

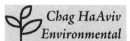
Chag HaAviv
Environmental

Chag HaPesach
Storytelling

Chag HaCheirut
Liberation

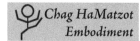
Chag HaMatzot
Embodiment

"And afflicted us" — as is is stated (Exodus 1:11); "And they placed upon him leaders over the work-tax in order to afflict them with their burdens; and they built storage cities, Pithom and Ra'amses."

"And put upon us hard work" — as it is stated (Exodus 1:11), "And they enslaved Bnei Yisrael with breaking work."

וַיְעַנּוּנוּ. כְּמָה שֶׁנֶּאֱמַר: וַיָּשִׂימוּ עָלָיו שָׂרֵי מִסִּים לְמַעַן עַנֹּתוֹ בְּסִבְלֹתָם. וַיִּבֶן עָרֵי מִסְכְּנוֹת לְפַרְעֹה. אֶת־פִּתֹם וְאֶת־רַעַמְסֵס. וַיִּתְּנוּ עָלֵינוּ עֲבֹדָה קָשָׁה. כְּמָה שֶׁנֶּאֱמַר: וַיַּעֲבִדוּ מִצְרַיִם אֶת־בְּנֵי יִשְׂרָאֵל בְּפָרֶךְ.

The Wealthy Jewish Communal Leaders (Izmir, 1847)

All of the expenses of the city, [including the cost of the] Society for Visiting and Tending to the Sick, the Burial Society, the Society for Clothing the Poor, the Talmud Torah school, the 'asara batlanim,' the chief rabbi, and the rabbinic court are covered by the *gabela* [internal Jewish communal tax instituted by community leaders under Ottoman rule] on wine, meat, and cheese. Of the 25,000 arayot yielded every year by the wine gabela, the poor and middle classes pay twenty thousand arayot, while the wealthy communal leaders pay five thousand. The same is true for meat. The poor cover the payments that are due the ritual slaughterers along with additional sums for the expenses of the city, nearing forty thousand arayot...As has been made known across the whole city, of the ninety thousand [arayot] yielded by the meat gabela per year, the poor and middle classes pay at least seventy thousand.

Such is the administration and rule of the wealthy communal leaders, who treat the poor as slaves, taking no pity on them and abusing them much more than [we were abused during] our enslavement in Egypt.

—Translated from Ladino by Dina Danon in *Sephardi Lives*

"And we we cried out to the Lord, the God of our ancestors, and the Lord heard our voice, and saw our affliction, our toil and our duress" (Deuteronomy 26:7).

"And we cried out to the Lord, the God of our ancestors" — as it is stated (Exodus 2:23); "And it was in those great days that the king of Egypt died and Bnei Yisrael sighed from the work and yelled out, and their supplication went up to God from the work."

וַנִּצְעַק אֶל יהוה אֱלֹהֵי אֲבֹתֵינוּ, וַיִּשְׁמַע יהוה אֶת־קֹלֵנוּ, וַיַּרְא אֶת־עָנְיֵנוּ וְאֶת עֲמָלֵנוּ וְאֶת לַחֲצֵנוּ. וַנִּצְעַק אֶל יהוה אֱלֹהֵי אֲבֹתֵינוּ — כְּמָה שֶׁנֶּאֱמַר: וַיְהִי בַיָּמִים הָרַבִּים הָהֵם וַיָּמָת מֶלֶךְ מִצְרַיִם, וַיֵּאָנְחוּ בְנֵי־יִשְׂרָאֵל מִן־הָעֲבוֹדָה וַיִּזְעָקוּ, וַתַּעַל שַׁוְעָתָם אֶל־הָאֱלֹהִים מִן הָעֲבֹדָה.

Four Stages In Connecting In Relationship

The Divrei Negidim commentary (Rabbi Yehudah Rosenberg, 1860–1936, Poland and Canada) points out that there are four terms used here for how God (Elohim) responds to the Israelites in Egypt. God heard their moaning; God *remembered* the covenant; God *saw* the Israelites; and God *knew*. Each of these verbs represents a stage in bridging the gap between God and people.

- Hearing is the first stage, and represents a focus of attention.
- Recalling is the second, where God remembers the covenantal relationship. This is focused on the past rather than the present.
- In the third stage, God sees the Israelites in their current situation, but focuses only on their external attributes.
- The final stage of knowing represents a fully developed connection. God recognizes the interior and the exterior experiences.

Does this process ring true to you? Does it fit with your relationships? What does it mean for God to have to go through a multi-stage process to reach humanity?

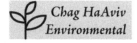
Chag HaAviv Environmental

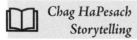
Chag HaPesach Storytelling

Chag HaCheirut Liberation

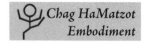
Chag HaMatzot Embodiment

"And the Lord heard our voice"
— as it is stated (Exodus 2:24-25);
"And God heard their groans and
God remembered the covenant
with Abraham and with Isaac and
with Jacob. God looked upon the
Israelites and God knew."

Hold up the charoset while reading this passage.

"And God saw our affliction" —
this [refers to] the separation from
the way of the world, as it is stated
(Exodus 2:25); "And God saw Bnei
Yisrael and God knew."

וַיִּשְׁמַע יהוה אֶת קֹלֵנוּ. כְּמָה
שֶׁנֶּאֱמַר: וַיִּשְׁמַע אֱלֹהִים אֶת־
נַאֲקָתָם, וַיִּזְכֹּר אֱלֹהִים אֶת־בְּרִיתוֹ
אֶת־אַבְרָהָם, אֶת־יִצְחָק וְאֶת־
יַעֲקֹב. וַיַּרְא אֱלֹהִים אֶת־בְּנֵי יִשְׂרָאֵל
וַיֵּדַע אֱלֹהִים.

וַיַּרְא אֶת־עָנְיֵנוּ. זוֹ פְּרִישׁוּת דֶּרֶךְ
אֶרֶץ, כְּמָה שֶׁנֶּאֱמַר: וַיַּרְא אֱלֹהִים
אֶת בְּנֵי־יִשְׂרָאֵל וַיֵּדַע אֱלֹהִים.

Reproductive Justice In Egypt

The midrash uses the euphemism "separation from the way of the world." This refers
to the ways the Egyptians tried to prevent the Israelites from engaging in intimate
relationships as a form of coerced birth control.

These midrashim are clear: not having agency over your own body and reproductive
choices is a form of slavery.

Resistance Under The Apple Trees

The Israelite slaves in Egypt had no agency over their bodies or intimate relationships. Midrashic stories share how the Egyptians tried to keep couples separate to dehumanize and demoralize the Israelites. There are many stories of resistance, including the discussion below from Pesachim 116a, about whether eating charoset at the seder is a mitzvah.

Rabbi Elazar, son of Rabbi Tzadok, says that eating charoset is a mitzvah. What is the nature of this mitzva?

Rabbi Levi says: It is in remembrance of the apple trees [where the Israelite women would entertain their lovers].

And Rabbi Yochanan says: The haroset is in remembrance of the mortar used by the Jews for their slave labor in Egypt.

Abaye said: Therefore, to fulfill both opinions, one must prepare it tart and one must prepare it thick. One must prepare it tart in remembrance of the apple, and one must prepare it thick in remembrance of the mortar.

רַבִּי אֶלְעָזָר בְּרַבִּי צָדוֹק אוֹמֵר מִצְוָה וְכוּ׳.

מַאי מִצְוָה?

רַבִּי לֵוִי אוֹמֵר: זֵכֶר לַתַּפּוּחַ.

וְרַבִּי יוֹחָנָן אוֹמֵר: זֵכֶר לַטִּיט.

אָמַר אַבָּיֵי: הִלְכָּךְ צָרִיךְ לְקַהוֹיֵיהּ וְצָרִיךְ לְסַמּוֹכֵיהּ.

לְקַהוֹיֵיהּ — זֵכֶר לַתַּפּוּחַ, וְצָרִיךְ לְסַמּוֹכֵיהּ — זֵכֶר לַטִּיט.

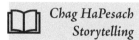
Chag HaAviv
Environmental

Chag HaPesach
Storytelling

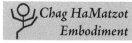
Chag HaCheirut
Liberation

Chag HaMatzot
Embodiment

The Apple Trees

The source of the story about the apple trees is Song of Songs 8:5:
>Under the apple tree I roused you;
>It was there your mother conceived you,
>There she who bore you conceived you.

The rabbis connect this line to the mothers in Egypt.

Archeological evidence suggests that apples originated in Kazakstan and traveled to the Middle East through trade routes. There were apples planted in Europe by 1500 BCE and in Egypt by 1300 BCE.

"And our toil" — this refers to the sons, as is stated (Exodus 1:15-17, 22): "The king of Egypt spoke to the Hebrew midwives, one of whom was named Shifrah and the other Puah, saying, "When you deliver the Hebrew women, look at the birthstones: if it is a boy, kill him; if it is a girl, let her live." The midwives, fearing God, did not do as the king of Egypt had told them; they let the boys live.

... Then Pharaoh charged all his people, saying, 'Every boy that is born you shall throw into the Nile, but let every girl live.'"

וְאֶת־עֲמָלֵנוּ. אֵלּוּ הַבָּנִים. כְּמָה שֶׁנֶּאֱמַר: וַיֹּאמֶר מֶלֶךְ מִצְרַיִם לַמְיַלְּדֹת הָעִבְרִיֹּת אֲשֶׁר שֵׁם הָאַחַת שִׁפְרָה וְשֵׁם הַשֵּׁנִית פּוּעָה: וַיֹּאמֶר בְּיַלֶּדְכֶן אֶת־הָעִבְרִיּוֹת וּרְאִיתֶן עַל־הָאָבְנָיִם אִם־בֵּן הוּא וַהֲמִתֶּן אֹתוֹ וְאִם־בַּת הִוא וָחָיָה: וַתִּירֶאןָ הַמְיַלְּדֹת אֶת־הָאֱלֹהִים וְלֹא עָשׂוּ כַּאֲשֶׁר דִּבֶּר אֲלֵיהֶן מֶלֶךְ מִצְרָיִם וַתְּחַיֶּיןָ אֶת־הַיְלָדִים: ...וַיְצַו פַּרְעֹה לְכָל־עַמּוֹ לֵאמֹר כָּל־הַבֵּן הַיִּלּוֹד הַיְאֹרָה תַּשְׁלִיכֻהוּ וְכָל־הַבַּת תְּחַיּוּן:

Civil Disobedience

Shifra and Puah choose to disobey Pharaoh. Instead, they follow their consciences and their relationship with God. When Pharaoh calls them in to ask why they are not following his orders, they make up a weak excuse. In response, Pharaoh extends his edict to the entire nation. All Egyptians, not just the midwives, are responsible for the murder of the Israelite baby boys.

The text is not clear whether the "Hebrew midwives" are themselves Israelites or whether they are just the midwives who serve the Israelite community. How is the story different if they are activists from within the Israelite community or Egyptians standing in solidarity?

When the midwives are ineffective, Pharaoh charges all Egyptian people with reporting their Israelite neighbors with young baby boys or throwing the babies into the Nile themselves. Given this context, was Shifra and Puah's civil disobedience effective? How can we fight for justice when the forces of evil are so powerful?

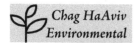
Chag HaAviv
Environmental

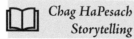
Chag HaPesach
Storytelling

Chag HaCheirut
Liberation

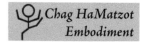
Chag HaMatzot
Embodiment

The Planted Babies

The Talmudic sage Rav Avira (Sotah 11b) taught that the actions of the righteous women in Egypt, surviving despite horrific violence, made the redemption from Egypt possible. He told the following story, which incorporates many of the texts in the Haggadah commentary:

When the women went into labor, they would give birth in the field under the apple tree, as it is stated: "Under the apple tree I awakened you; there your mother was in travail with you; there was she in travail and brought you forth" (Song of Songs 8:5). The Holy Blessed One would send an angel from the heavens to help clean and prepare the newborns...

And the angel would prepare for them two round stones, one from oil and one from honey for the babies to nurse. As it is written, "And God would suckle them with honey from a crag and oil from a flinty rock."

Once the Egyptians noticed that there were Jewish babies, they would come to kill them. But a miracle would occur, and they would be absorbed by the earth. The Egyptians would bring oxen and would plow upon them...After the Egyptians left, the babies would emerge and exit the ground like grass of the field, as it is stated: "I caused you to increase even as the growth of the field" (Ezekiel 16:7).

As the babies grew, they would come like many flocks of sheep to their homes, as it is stated: "And you did increase and grow up and you came with excellent beauty [ba'adi adayim]" (ibid). Do not read the verse as: "Ba'adi adayim," "with excellent beauty." Rather, read it as: Be'edrei adarim, meaning: As many flocks.

When the Holy Blessed One revealed Godself at the Red Sea, these children recognized God first, as it is stated: "This is my God, who I will glorify" (Exodus 15:2).

וְכֵיוָן שֶׁמַּגִּיעַ זְמַן מוֹלְדֵיהֶן הוֹלְכוֹת וְיוֹלְדוֹת בַּשָּׂדֶה תַּחַת הַתַּפּוּחַ שֶׁנֶּאֱמַר תַּחַת הַתַּפּוּחַ עוֹרַרְתִּיךָ וְגוֹ׳. וְהַקָּדוֹשׁ בָּרוּךְ הוּא שׁוֹלֵחַ מִשְּׁמֵי מָרוֹם מִי שֶׁמְּנַקֵּיר וּמְשַׁפֵּיר אוֹתָן...

וּמְלַקֵּט לָהֶן שְׁנֵי עִגּוּלִין אֶחָד שֶׁל שֶׁמֶן וְאֶחָד שֶׁל דְּבַשׁ שֶׁנֶּאֱמַר וַיֵּנִקֵהוּ דְבַשׁ מִסֶּלַע וְשֶׁמֶן וְגוֹ׳.

וְכֵיוָן שֶׁמַּכִּירִין בָּהֶן מִצְרִיִּים בָּאִין לְהוֹרְגָן וְנַעֲשָׂה לָהֶם נֵס וְנִבְלָעִין בַּקַּרְקַע וּמְבִיאִין שְׁוָורִים וְחוֹרְשִׁין עַל גַּבָּן... לְאַחַר שֶׁהוֹלְכִין הָיוּ מְבַצְבְּצִין וְיוֹצְאִין כְּעֵשֶׂב הַשָּׂדֶה שֶׁנֶּאֱמַר רְבָבָה כְּצֶמַח הַשָּׂדֶה נְתַתִּיךְ.

וְכֵיוָן שֶׁמִּתְגַּדְּלִין בָּאִין עֲדָרִים עֲדָרִים לְבָתֵּיהֶן שֶׁנֶּאֱמַר וַתִּרְבִּי וַתִּגְדְּלִי וַתָּבֹאִי בַּעֲדִי עֲדָיִים אַל תִּקְרֵי בַּעֲדִי עֲדָיִים אֶלָּא בְּעֶדְרֵי עֲדָרִים.

וּכְשֶׁנִּגְלָה הַקָּדוֹשׁ בָּרוּךְ הוּא עַל הַיָּם הֵם הִכִּירוּהוּ תְּחִלָּה שֶׁנֶּאֱמַר זֶה אֵלִי וְאַנְוֵהוּ.

"And our duress" — this [refers to] the pressure, as it is stated (Exodus 3:9); "And I also saw the duress that the Egyptians are applying on them."

וְאֶת לַחֲצֵנוּ. זוֹ הַדְּחַק, כְּמָה שֶׁנֶּאֱמַר: וְגַם־רָאִיתִי אֶת־הַלַּחַץ אֲשֶׁר מִצְרַיִם לֹחֲצִים אֹתָם.

All It Did Not Take Away

Modernism thrived in Paris in the early part of the twentieth century. At the time, the English and United States governments actively repressed and persecuted artists and writers for "obscenity" and deviation from social norms. In contrast, Paris became a place where freethinkers could connect, live freely, and make art. Gertrude Stein wrote, "Paris was where the twentieth century was," "the place that suited those of us that were to create the twentieth century art and literature." It was not just a matter of what Paris provided, but "it was all it did not take away."

Bread and Roses

In the early 1910s, labor activists fought for better working conditions and the vote for women. Several strikes used the slogan "Bread for all, And Roses too." Labor activist Rose Schneiderman (1882–1972) elaborated on this theme in a speech in Cleveland in 1912:

"What the woman who labors wants is the right to live, not simply exist — the right to life as the rich woman has the right to life, and the sun and music and art. You have nothing that the humblest worker has not a right to have also. The worker must have bread, but she must have roses, too."

When we consider the pressure and duress in Egypt and today, do we consider limited access to "sun and music and art" as part of the oppression?

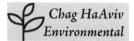 *Chag HaAviv* Environmental

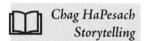 *Chag HaPesach* Storytelling

 *Chag HaCheirut* Liberation

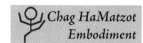 *Chag HaMatzot* Embodiment

"And the Lord took us out of Egypt with a strong hand and with an outstretched forearm and with great awe and with signs and with wonders" (Deuteronomy 26:8).

"And the Lord took us out of Egypt" — not through an angel and not through a seraph and not through a messenger, but directly by the Holy Blessed One God's self, as it is stated (Exodus 12:12): "And I will pass through the Land of Egypt on that night and I will smite every firstborn in the Land of Egypt, from humans to animals; and with all the gods of Egypt, I will make judgments, I am the Lord."

וַיּוֹצִאֵנוּ יהוה מִמִּצְרַיִם בְּיָד חֲזָקָה, וּבִזְרֹעַ נְטוּיָה, וּבְמֹרָא גָּדֹל, וּבְאֹתוֹת וּבְמֹפְתִים.
וַיּוֹצִאֵנוּ יהוה מִמִּצְרַיִם. לֹא עַל־יְדֵי מַלְאָךְ, וְלֹא עַל־יְדֵי שָׂרָף, וְלֹא עַל־יְדֵי שָׁלִיחַ, אֶלָּא הַקָּדוֹשׁ בָּרוּךְ הוּא בִּכְבוֹדוֹ וּבְעַצְמוֹ. שֶׁנֶּאֱמַר: וְעָבַרְתִּי בְאֶרֶץ מִצְרַיִם בַּלַּיְלָה הַזֶּה, וְהִכֵּיתִי כָל־בְּכוֹר בְּאֶרֶץ מִצְרַיִם מֵאָדָם וְעַד בְּהֵמָה, וּבְכָל אֱלֹהֵי מִצְרַיִם אֶעֱשֶׂה שְׁפָטִים. אֲנִי יהוה.

I Will Make Judgments, I Am The Lord

God carries out the Tenth Plague. Unlike Pharaoh, who mandates that all male babies must be killed and then deputizes the midwives and later his armies to act on it, God does not hide behind a messenger.

"And I will pass through the Land of Egypt" — I and not an angel.

"And I will smite every firstborn" — I and not a seraph. "And with all the gods of Egypt, I will make judgments" — I and not a messenger. "I am the Lord" — I am God and there is no other.

וְעָבַרְתִּי בְאֶרֶץ מִצְרַיִם בַּלַּיְלָה הַזֶּה - אֲנִי וְלֹא מַלְאָךְ; וְהִכֵּיתִי כָל בְּכוֹר בְּאֶרֶץ־מִצְרַיִם. אֲנִי וְלֹא שָׂרָף; וּבְכָל־אֱלֹהֵי מִצְרַיִם אֶעֱשֶׂה שְׁפָטִים. אֲנִי וְלֹא הַשָּׁלִיחַ; אֲנִי יהוה. אֲנִי הוּא וְלֹא אַחֵר.

Another interpretation: "And I will smite every firstborn." As it is stated (Exodus 12:29-30), "In the middle of the night the Lord struck down all the first-born in the land of Egypt, from the first-born of Pharaoh who sat on the throne to the first-born of the captive who was in the dungeon, and all the first-born of the cattle. And Pharaoh arose in the night, with all his courtiers and all the Egyptians—because there was a loud cry in Egypt; for there was no house where there was not someone dead."

דָּבָר אַחֵר: וְהִכֵּיתִי כָל־בְּכוֹר בְּאֶרֶץ מִצְרַיִם. כְּמָה שֶׁנֶּאֱמַר: וַיְהִי בַּחֲצִי הַלַּיְלָה וַיהוָה הִכָּה כָל־בְּכוֹר בְּאֶרֶץ מִצְרַיִם מִבְּכֹר פַּרְעֹה הַיֹּשֵׁב עַל־כִּסְאוֹ עַד בְּכוֹר הַשְּׁבִי אֲשֶׁר בְּבֵית הַבּוֹר וְכֹל בְּכוֹר בְּהֵמָה. וַיָּקָם פַּרְעֹה לַיְלָה הוּא וְכָל־עֲבָדָיו וְכָל־מִצְרַיִם וַתְּהִי צְעָקָה גְדֹלָה בְּמִצְרָיִם כִּי־אֵין בַּיִת אֲשֶׁר אֵין־שָׁם מֵת.

Why the First Born?

Some commentators note that the Torah believes Egyptian society valued primogeniture. First born Egyptians would have significant social status and control over their families and younger siblings. The death of the first born removes that social hierachy and challenges Egypt to rebuild a more just system.

The Captive in the Dungeon and Collective Punishment

All Egyptian first born children die in the tenth plague, "from the prince on his throne to the child of the captive in the dungeon." The Hebrew word for dungeon here is "bor." The same word is used in Joseph's capitivity in Egypt. This parallel reminds us that we, too, started our experience in Egypt in the dungeon. Even as Bnei Yisrael are able to leave for freedom, there are still others who still suffer, both at the hands of the Egyptians and through God's collective punishment.

Embodied Grief

The Egyptians' grief is felt in their bodies. The entire nation is awakened in the middle of the night. Something feels wrong. The discovery of all the death and loss prompts a spontaneous, collective outcry. Every household has lost someone.

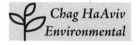 *Chag HaAviv* Environmental

 *Chag HaPesach* Storytelling

 *Chag HaCheirut* Liberation

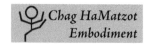 *Chag HaMatzot* Embodiment

"With a strong hand and with an outstretched arm" — this [refers to] the lovingkindness, as it is stated (Pslams 136:12): "With a strong hand and with an outstretched arm, for God's lovingkindness lasts forever."

Another interpretation: "With a strong hand and with an outstretched arm"—this [refers to] the fury, as it is stated (Ezekiel 20:33): "As I live— declares the Lord God—I will reign over you with a strong hand, and with an outstretched arm, and with overflowing fury."

בְּיָד חֲזָקָה וּבִזְרֹעַ נְטוּיָה. זוֹ הַחֶסֶד, כְּמָה שֶׁנֶּאֱמַר: בְּיָד חֲזָקָה וּבִזְרוֹעַ נְטוּיָה כִּי לְעוֹלָם חַסְדּוֹ.
דָּבָר אַחֵר: בְּיָד חֲזָקָה וּבִזְרֹעַ נְטוּיָה. זוֹ הַחֵמָה, כְּמָה שֶׁנֶּאֱמַר: חַי־אָנִי נְאֻם אֲדֹנָי יְהוִה אִם־לֹא בְּיָד חֲזָקָה וּבִזְרוֹעַ נְטוּיָה וּבְחֵמָה שְׁפוּכָה אֶמְלוֹךְ עֲלֵיכֶם:

Tzedek Versus Chesed
Justice Versus Lovingkindness

This midrash highlights the tensions between justice and lovingkindness, righteous anger and revenge. Where do God's actions in the Passover story fall within those categories? How should society respond when lovingkindness for one person might mean harshness and pain for another? Are justice and lovingkindness really in tension? Is there space for accountability within lovingkindness?

THE TRADITIONAL TEXT

This is a slight departure from the traditional midrash in this section. The traditional text here reads:

בְּיָד חֲזָקָה. זוֹ הַדֶּבֶר, כְּמָה שֶׁנֶּאֱמַר: הִנֵּה יַד־ יהוה הוֹיָה בְּמִקְנְךָ אֲשֶׁר בַּשָּׂדֶה, בַּסּוּסִים, בַּחֲמֹרִים, בַּגְּמַלִים, בַּבָּקָר וּבַצֹּאן, דֶּבֶר כָּבֵד מְאֹד.
וּבִזְרֹעַ נְטוּיָה. זוֹ הַחֶרֶב, כְּמָה שֶׁנֶּאֱמַר: וְחַרְבּוֹ שְׁלוּפָה בְּיָדוֹ, נְטוּיָה עַל־יְרוּשָׁלָיִם.

"With a strong hand" — this [refers to] the pestilence, as it is stated (Exodus 9:3); "Behold the hand of the Lord is upon your herds that are in the field, upon the horses, upon the donkeys, upon the camels, upon the cattle and upon the flocks, [there will be] a very heavy pestilence."

"And with an outstretched forearm" — this [refers to] the sword, as it is stated (I Chronicles 21:16); "And God's sword was drawn in God's hand, leaning over Jerusalem."

"And with great awe" — this [refers to the revelation of] the Divine Presence, as it is stated (Deuteronomy 4:34), "Or did God try to take a nation from within a nation with enigmas, with signs and with wonders and with war and with a strong hand and with an outstretched forearm and with great and awesome acts, like all that the Lord, your God, did for you in Egypt in front of your eyes?"

וּבְמוֹרָא גָדֹל. זוֹ גִּלּוּי שְׁכִינָה. כְּמָה שֶׁנֶּאֱמַר, אוֹ הֲנִסָּה אֱלֹהִים לָבוֹא לָקַחַת לוֹ גוֹי מִקֶּרֶב גּוֹי בְּמַסֹּת בְּאֹתֹת וּבְמוֹפְתִים וּבְמִלְחָמָה וּבְיָד חֲזָקָה וּבִזְרוֹעַ נְטוּיָה וּבְמוֹרָאִים גְּדֹלִים כְּכֹל אֲשֶׁר־עָשָׂה לָכֶם יְהוָה אֱלֹהֵיכֶם בְּמִצְרַיִם לְעֵינֶיךָ.

Hands, Arms, Anthropomorphism, and Miracles

God is repeatedly described as responding to Egypt with a "strong hand" and "outstretched arm." Are these different images, or different ways of describing the same thing? Why do we use such anthropomorphic language?

God directs Moses to take his staff in his hand to perform miracles. What is the role of the staff? Why does God specify to take it "in your hand"?

"And with signs" — this [refers to] the staff, as it is stated (Exodus 4:17); "And this staff you shall take in your hand, that with it you will perform signs."

וּבְאֹתוֹת. זֶה הַמַּטֶּה, כְּמָה שֶׁנֶּאֱמַר: וְאֶת הַמַּטֶּה הַזֶּה תִּקַּח בְּיָדְךָ, אֲשֶׁר תַּעֲשֶׂה־בּוֹ אֶת הָאֹתוֹת.

Chag HaAviv
Environmental

Chag HaPesach
Storytelling

Chag HaCheirut
Liberation

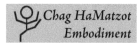
Chag HaMatzot
Embodiment

"And with wonders" — this refers to the blood, as it is stated (Joel 3:3); "And I will place my wonders in the skies and in the earth, blood and fire and pillars of smoke."

וּבְמֹפְתִים. זֶה הַדָּם, כְּמָה שֶׁנֶּאֱמַר: וְנָתַתִּי מוֹפְתִים בַּשָּׁמַיִם וּבָאָרֶץ, דָּם וָאֵשׁ וְתִימְרוֹת עָשָׁן.

The Rotting Fish

Chizkuni (c. 1220–1260, France) teaches in his commentary on Exodus 7:20:

לא נעשה היאור דם כי אם לפי שעה ומיד מתה הדגה מחמת הדם ואחר כך חזר היאור לקדמותו

The Nile only became blood briefly. The fish died immediately from the blood, and afterwards the water returned to normal.

Chizkuni goes on to explain that when the text states that the Egyptians were unable to drink the water for a much longer period, it was not because the river was blood. Rather, it was because the Nile was so polluted from the dead and rotting fish.

In this midrash, do you think God's goal is a show of power or to kill the fish and pollute the water? In our world today, how do we pollute the environment even long after we stop acting? What will we sacrifice for power? What "side effects" are we willing to tolerate?

Another explanation: "With a strong hand" corresponds to two plagues; "and with an outstretched forearm" corresponds to two plagues; "and with great awe" corresponds to two plagues; "and with signs" corresponds to two plagues; "and with wonders" corresponds to two plagues.

דָּבָר אַחֵר:
בְּיָד חֲזָקָה שְׁתַּיִם,
וּבִזְרֹעַ נְטוּיָה שְׁתַּיִם,
וּבְמֹרָא גָדֹל, שְׁתַּיִם,
וּבְאֹתוֹת, שְׁתַּיִם,
וּבְמֹפְתִים, שְׁתַּיִם.

These are the ten plagues that the Holy Blessed One brought on the Egyptians in Egypt and they are:

אֵלּוּ עֶשֶׂר מַכּוֹת שֶׁהֵבִיא הַקָּדוֹשׁ בָּרוּךְ הוּא עַל־הַמִּצְרִים בְּמִצְרַיִם, וְאֵלּוּ הֵן:

Remove a drop of wine or grape juice from your cup with each plague.

Blood	דָּם
Frogs	צְפַרְדֵּעַ
Lice	כִּנִּים
Wild beasts	עָרוֹב
Pestilence	דֶּבֶר
Boils	שְׁחִין
Hail	בָּרָד
Locusts	אַרְבֶּה
Darkness	חֹשֶׁךְ
Death of the First Born	מַכַּת בְּכוֹרוֹת

רַבִּי יְהוּדָה הָיָה נוֹתֵן בָּהֶם סִמָּנִים:
דְּצַ"ךְ עַדַ"שׁ בְּאַחַ"ב.

Rabbi Yehuda made a mnemonic (from the first letters of each plague):
Detzach, adash, beachav.

In English: BeFeL, WePuB, HeLDaD

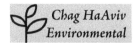 Chag HaAviv Environmental
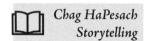 Chag HaPesach Storytelling
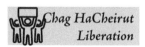 Chag HaCheirut Liberation
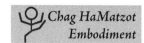 Chag HaMatzot Embodiment

Dayenu! ‏דַּיֵּנוּ!

כַּמָה מַעֲלוֹת טוֹבוֹת לַמָּקוֹם עָלֵינוּ!

דַּיֵּנוּ.	וְלֹא עָשָׂה בָהֶם שְׁפָטִים,	אִלּוּ הוֹצִיאָנוּ מִמִּצְרַיִם,
דַּיֵּנוּ.	וְלֹא עָשָׂה בֵאלֹהֵיהֶם,	אִלּוּ עָשָׂה בָהֶם שְׁפָטִים,
דַּיֵּנוּ.	וְלֹא הָרַג אֶת־בְּכוֹרֵיהֶם,	אִלּוּ עָשָׂה בֵאלֹהֵיהֶם,
דַּיֵּנוּ.	וְלֹא נָתַן לָנוּ אֶת־מָמוֹנָם,	אִלּוּ הָרַג אֶת־בְּכוֹרֵיהֶם,
דַּיֵּנוּ.	וְלֹא קָרַע לָנוּ אֶת־הַיָּם,	אִלּוּ נָתַן לָנוּ אֶת־מָמוֹנָם,
דַּיֵּנוּ.	וְלֹא הֶעֱבִירָנוּ בְּתוֹכוֹ בֶּחָרָבָה,	אִלּוּ קָרַע לָנוּ אֶת־הַיָּם,
דַּיֵּנוּ.	וְלֹא שִׁקַּע צָרֵנוּ בְּתוֹכוֹ,	אִלּוּ הֶעֱבִירָנוּ בְּתוֹכוֹ בֶּחָרָבָה,
דַּיֵּנוּ.	וְלֹא סִפֵּק צָרְכֵּנוּ בַּמִּדְבָּר 40 שָׁנָה,	אִלּוּ שִׁקַּע צָרֵנוּ בְּתוֹכוֹ,
דַּיֵּנוּ.	וְלֹא הֶאֱכִילָנוּ אֶת־הַמָּן,	אִלּוּ סִפֵּק צָרְכֵּנוּ בַּמִּדְבָּר 40 שָׁנָה,
דַּיֵּנוּ.	וְלֹא נָתַן לָנוּ אֶת־הַשַּׁבָּת,	אִלּוּ הֶאֱכִילָנוּ אֶת־הַמָּן,
דַּיֵּנוּ.	וְלֹא קֵרְבָנוּ לִפְנֵי הַר סִינַי,	אִלּוּ נָתַן לָנוּ אֶת־הַשַּׁבָּת,
דַּיֵּנוּ.	וְלֹא נַתַן לָנוּ אֶת־הַתּוֹרָה,	אִלּוּ קֵרְבָנוּ לִפְנֵי הַר סִינַי,
דַּיֵּנוּ.	וְלֹא הִכְנִיסָנוּ לְאֶרֶץ יִשְׂרָאֵל,	אִלּוּ נַתַן לָנוּ אֶת־הַתּוֹרָה,
דַּיֵּנוּ.	וְלֹא בָנָה לָנוּ אֶת־בֵּית הַבְּחִירָה,	אִלּוּ הִכְנִיסָנוּ לְאֶרֶץ יִשְׂרָאֵל,

How many steps of goodness has The Place [God] given us!

If God had rescued us from Egypt,
   but did not judge the Egyptians, *dayenu* [it would have been enough].
If God had judged the Egyptians, but did not judge their gods, *dayenu*.
If God had judged their gods, but did not kill their firstborns, *dayenu*.
If God had killed their firstborns, but did not give us their reparations, *dayenu*.
If God had given us their reparations, but did not split the Red Sea, *dayenu*.
If God had split the Red Sea, but did not bring us across on dry land, *dayenu*.
If God had brought us across, but did not drown our oppressors in it, *dayenu*.
If God had drowned our oppressors,
   but did not care for us in the wilderness for forty years, *dayenu*.
If God had taken care of us in the wilderness, but had not fed us the manna, *dayenu*.
If God had fed us the manna, but did not give us Shabbat, *dayenu*.
If God had given us Shabbat, but did not bring us to Mount Sinai, *dayenu*.
If God had brought us to Mount Sinai, but did not give us the Torah, *dayenu*.
If God had given us the Torah, but not brought us to the Land of Israel, *dayenu*.
If God had brought us to the Land of Israel, but not built for us the Temple, *dayenu*.
DAYENU. DAI DAI DAYENU, DAI DAI DAYENU.

How much more so is the good that is doubled and quadrupled that The Place has given us!

Since God took us out of Egypt, and made judgments with them, and made judgements with their gods, and killed their firstborns, and gave us their money as reparations, and split the Red Sea for us, and brought us through it on dry land, and drowned our oppressors in the sea, and took care of us in the wilderness for forty years, and fed us the manna, and gave us the Shabbat, and brought us close to Mount Sinai, and gave us the Torah, and brought us into the land of Israel and built us the Temple to atone for all of our sins.

עַל אַחַת, כַּמָּה וְכַמָּה, טוֹבָה כְפוּלָה וּמְכֻפֶּלֶת לַמָּקוֹם עָלֵינוּ: שֶׁהוֹצִיאָנוּ מִמִּצְרַיִם, וְעָשָׂה בָהֶם שְׁפָטִים, וְעָשָׂה בֵאלֹהֵיהֶם, וְהָרַג אֶת־בְּכוֹרֵיהֶם, וְנָתַן לָנוּ אֶת־מָמוֹנָם, וְקָרַע לָנוּ אֶת־הַיָּם, וְהֶעֱבִירָנוּ בְּתוֹכוֹ בֶּחָרָבָה, וְשִׁקַּע צָרֵנוּ בְּתוֹכוֹ, וְסִפֵּק צָרְכֵּנוּ בַּמִּדְבָּר אַרְבָּעִים שָׁנָה, וְהֶאֱכִילָנוּ אֶת־הַמָּן, וְנָתַן לָנוּ אֶת־הַשַּׁבָּת, וְקֵרְבָנוּ לִפְנֵי הַר סִינַי, וְנָתַן לָנוּ אֶת־הַתּוֹרָה, וְהִכְנִיסָנוּ לְאֶרֶץ יִשְׂרָאֵל, וּבָנָה לָנוּ אֶת־בֵּית הַבְּחִירָה לְכַפֵּר עַל־כָּל־עֲווֹנוֹתֵינוּ.

What Is Enough?

Would it really have been enough if God had taken us out of Egypt, but left us to be recaptured at the Red Sea? Would it really have been enough if God had brought us through the desert, but didn't give us the Torah at Mount Sinai?

One answer connects dayenu to Hallel, from listing the miracles to giving praise. In this view, dayenu does not mean "it would be enough" period, it means "it would be sufficient for us to give praise."

This applies both to gratitude for God's actions and to actions in our own lives. So many problems and injustices seem intractable and overwhelming. Even so, each little step moves us forward toward liberation and redemption.

Many haggadot continue with Rabban Gamliel's discussion of Pesach, Matzah, and Maror here. You can find this discussion on pages 71–74, when we eat the matzah, maror, and koreich sandwich.

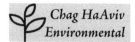
Chag HaAviv
Environmental

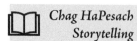
Chag HaPesach
Storytelling

Chag HaCheirut
Liberation

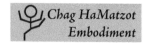
Chag HaMatzot
Embodiment

Kos Miriam/Miriam's Cup

Ten things were created at twilight
just before the first Shabbat.
They are:
the mouth of the earth
(that swallowed Korach);
the mouth of Miriam's well;
the mouth of the donkey
(that spoke to Balaam);
the original rainbow;
the manna;
the staff;
the *shamir* [mythic worm which
chiseled the Ten Commandments];
the letters;
the writing;
and the tablets.
Some add the mazikin
[demonic spirits]...
some add the first tongs which were
needed to make all the other tongs.
(Pirkei Avot 5:6)

עֲשָׂרָה דְבָרִים נִבְרְאוּ בְּעֶרֶב שַׁבָּת
בֵּין הַשְּׁמָשׁוֹת,
וְאֵלוּ הֵן,
פִּי הָאָרֶץ,
וּפִי הַבְּאֵר,
וּפִי הָאָתוֹן,
וְהַקֶּשֶׁת,
וְהַמָּן,
וְהַמַּטֶּה,
וְהַשָּׁמִיר,
וְהַכְּתָב,
וְהַמִּכְתָּב,
וְהַלּוּחוֹת.

וְיֵשׁ אוֹמְרִים, אַף הַמַּזִּיקִין...
וְיֵשׁ אוֹמְרִים,
אַף צְבָת בִּצְבָת עֲשׂוּיָה.

Beyn Hashmashot/At Twilight

Twilight—the time at sunset before the sun is fully set—is a time of great holiness and possibility. Judaism celebrates these times between. There is power in the liminality, the in-betweenness. God created magic during the twilight before the first Shabbat.

If you could have created anything during that in-between time, what would you have created?

What might Miriam have created then?

Fill Miriam's cup with seltzer water to symbolize the mayim hayyim, the living waters. All say:

This is Miriam's cup,
the cup of living waters,
to remember the Exodus from Egypt.

זֹאת כּוֹס מִרְיָם,
כּוֹס מַיִם חַיִּים,
זֵכֶר לִיצִיאַת מִצְרָיִם.

At Blackwater Pond

At Blackwater Pond the tossed waters have settled
after a night of rain.
I dip my cupped hands. I drink
a long time. It tastes
like stone, leaves, fire. It falls cold
into my body, waking the bones. I hear them
deep inside me, whispering
oh what is that beautiful thing
that just happened?

—Mary Oliver

For all forty years in the desert, Bnei Yisrael had a traveling well because of the merit of Miriam, as it is stated, (Numbers 20:1-2) "Miriam died there and was buried there. And the community did not have water."

כָּל אַרְבָּעִים שָׁנָה הָיָה לִבְנֵי יִשְׂרָאֵל הַבְּאֵר בִּזְכוּת מִרְיָם. כְּמָה שֶׁנֶּאֱמַר, וַתָּמָת שָׁם מִרְיָם וַתִּקָּבֵר שָׁם. וְלֹא־הָיָה מַיִם לָעֵדָה.

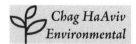
Chag HaAviv
Environmental

Chag HaPesach
Storytelling

Chag HaCheirut
Liberation

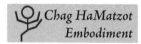
Chag HaMatzot
Embodiment

And such was the well
which accompanied Israel in the
wilderness:
like a rock full of holes as a sieve,
bubbling and rising as from the
mouth of this flask;
ascending with them to the
mountains and descending with them
to the valleys;
wherever Israel would rest,
it resting opposite them,
a high place opposite the entrance to
the Tent of Meeting.
The princes of Israel would come and
encircle it with their staffs,
and recite over it this song:
"Rise up, O well! Sing out to it!
Rise up, O well! Sing out to it!"
(Numbers 21:17)

—*Tosefta Sukkah 3:3*

וְכָךְ הָיְתָה הַבְּאֵר
שֶׁהָיְתָה עִם יִשְׂרָאֵל בַּמִּדְבָּר:
דּוֹמָה לְסֶלַע מָלֵא כִבְרָה,
מְפַכְפֶּכֶת וְעוֹלָה כְּמִפִּי הַפַּךְ הַזֶּה.
עוֹלָה עִמָּהֶן לֶהָרִים,
וְיוֹרֶדֶת עִמָּהֶן לַגֵּאָיוֹת.
מָקוֹם שֶׁיִּשְׂרָאֵל שׁוֹרִין,
הִיא שׁוֹרָה כְּנֶגְדָן,
מָקוֹם גָּבוֹהַּ
כְּנֶגֶד פִּתְחוֹ שֶׁלְאֹהֶל מוֹעֵד.
נְשִׂיאֵי יִשְׂרָאֵל
בָּאִין וְסוֹבְבִין אוֹתָהּ בְּמַקְלוֹתֵיהֶן,
וְאוֹמֵר עָלֶיהָ אֶת הַשִּׁירָה:
עֲלִי בְאֵר, עֲנוּ לָהּ!
עֲלִי בְאֵר, עֲנוּ לָהּ!

Sustenance on Our Journeys

Miriam's well traveled with Bnei Yisrael throughout their entire journey in the wilderness, in good times and bad times, in hills and in valleys.
What do you bring with you in your travels? What sustains you?
The princes of Israel would honor the well by dancing and singing around it.
How do you honor what sustains you?

Rabbi Yochanan said: From the well...came most of their [Bnei Yisrael while they wandered in the desert] pleasure was from there, as Rabbi Yochanan said: The well would produce for them types of vegetation, types of grains, types of trees.

—*Shir HaShirim Rabbah 4:12*

רַבִּי יוֹחָנָן אָמַר: מִן הַבְּאֵר... הָיוּ
רֹב הֲנָיָתָן, דְּאָמַר רַבִּי יוֹחָנָן הַבְּאֵר
הָיְתָה מַעֲלָה לָהֶם מִינֵי דְשָׁאִים, מִינֵי
זֵרְעוֹנִים, מִינֵי אִילָנוֹת

A Traveling Oasis

Miriam's well is described less as a well and more as a traveling oasis—a porous rock that exudes water and grows plants for eating and green space for relaxation. A diversity of plants, grains, and trees travel with her. She does not just sate the thirst of her people in the desert; she also feeds and nourishes them, and provides a verdant rest stop.

How does the image of Miriam's well as an oasis change her role in the desert? Why does the text specify that the oasis contained a diversity of plants?

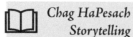 Chag HaAviv
Environmental

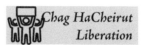 Chag HaPesach
Storytelling

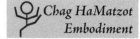 Chag HaCheirut
Liberation

Chag HaMatzot
Embodiment

Seeing Ourselves Leaving Egypt

In each and every generation, everyone is obligated to see themselves as if they left Egypt, as it is stated (Exodus 13:8); "And you shall explain to your child on that day: For the sake of this, did the Lord do [this] for me in my going out of Egypt." Not only our ancestors did the Holy Blessed One redeem, but rather also we too were redeemed, as it is stated (Deuteronomy 6:23); "And God took us out from there, in order to bring us in, to give us the land which was sworn to our ancestors."

בְּכָל־דּוֹר וָדוֹר חַיָּב אָדָם לִרְאוֹת אֶת־עַצְמוֹ כְּאִלּוּ הוּא יָצָא מִמִּצְרַיִם, שֶׁנֶּאֱמַר: וְהִגַּדְתָּ לְבִנְךָ בַּיּוֹם הַהוּא לֵאמֹר, בַּעֲבוּר זֶה עָשָׂה יהוה לִי בְּצֵאתִי מִמִּצְרָיִם. לֹא אֶת־אֲבוֹתֵינוּ בִּלְבָד גָּאַל הַקָּדוֹשׁ בָּרוּךְ הוּא, אֶלָּא אַף אוֹתָנוּ גָּאַל עִמָּהֶם, שֶׁנֶּאֱמַר: וְאוֹתָנוּ הוֹצִיא מִשָּׁם, לְמַעַן הָבִיא אוֹתָנוּ, לָתֶת לָנוּ אֶת־הָאָרֶץ אֲשֶׁר נִשְׁבַּע לַאֲבֹתֵינוּ.

Healing Through Embracing My Trans Body

I was steadily reaching in the dark across a chasm that separated who I was and who I thought I should be. Somewhere along the way, I grew weary of grasping at possible selves, just out of reach. So I put my arms down and wrapped them around me. I began healing by embracing myself through foreboding darkness until sunrise shone on my face. Eventually, I emerged, and surrendered to the brilliance, discovering truth, beauty, and peace that was already mine.

—Janet Mock, *Redefining Realness*

Transforming, Not Leaving

In the Pesach story, we leave Egypt and its narrowness to achieve freedom and redemption. However, there are other ways to create a flourishing ecosystem for all of us to thrive. When the U.S. National Park Service reintroduced wolves to Yellowstone Park in 1995, the wolves began to hunt weaker elk and bison, keeping the overall populations healthier. Fewer grazers meant willow and aspen trees could grow, creating new habitats. When ecologists in Exmoor, England released beavers onto land that had not had them in centuries, the beavers created a wetland within months of their arrival. Kingfishers and other birds moved in, as did amphibians, bats, and insects.

Sometimes freedom and redemption means leaving somewhere oppressive and forging a new path. Sometimes, to truly thrive, we need to bring in a new voice, a new energy, new vision, and new life—to utterly transform the environment in which we live.

None Of Us Are Free Until We Are All Free

I do not hesitate to say that our national defect is that we are not "tribal" enough; we have not sufficient solidarity to perceive that when the life and property of a Jew in the uttermost provinces of the Caucasus are attacked, the dignity of a Jew in free America is humiliated.

We who are prosperous and independent have not sufficient homogeneity to champion on the ground of a common creed, common stock, a common history, a common heritage of misfortune, the rights of the lowest and poorest Jew-peddler who flees, for life and liberty of thought, from Slavonic mobs. Until we are all free, we are none of us free.

—Emma Lazarus (1883)

To Make Ourselves Seen As Those Who Left Egypt

Another version of the text reads:
בְּכָל־דּוֹר וָדוֹר חַיָּב אָדָם לְהַרְאוֹת אֶת־עַצְמוֹ

In each and every generation, everyone is obligated to make themselves seen...

HIAS, the refugee assistance organization, was founded in 1881 as the Hebrew Immigrant Aid Society to assist immigrants and refugees because they were Jews. Today, HIAS helps refugees all around the world not because they are (necessarily) Jews, but because we are Jews.

What is the difference between privately thinking of ourselves as among those who left Egypt to deliberately making ourselves seen as a nation of refugees?

Chag HaAviv Environmental

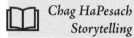
Chag HaPesach Storytelling

Chag HaCheirut Liberation

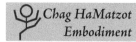
Chag HaMatzot Embodiment

Seeing Ourselves In Our Ancestors Who Left Egypt

The One Who Knew How To Walk Into Deep Water

My name is Nachshon. You might know me as Aminadav's son or Aaron's brother in law. My father is Aminadav, and my sister Elisheva is married to Aaron. But "son" and "brother in law" don't quite roll off my tongue.

As a child, I always liked hearing about my ancestors, especially about Grandpa Jacob when he was young. They said he was quiet and spent time in tents. I thought I was like him—I, too, preferred the company of my mother and the other women. But as I grew, I realized I was more like Grandma Leah, another quiet presence with uncanny vision and insight. A woman whose gifts were poorly understood and who sometimes inspired fear.

My sister Elisheva understood. Shortly after she started her apprenticeship with Yocheved the Midwife, she started bringing me mixtures and poultices—garlic, sesame, other herbs— which helped me grow into my body and my strength.

Navigating the chaos of the plagues and Pharaoh's increasing harshness among the women in the tents and among my family was challenging, but I made out alright.

When we reached the Red Sea, with the water in front of us and our oppressors' hoofbeats growing louder behind us, I saw Moses trembling. I saw my brother in law Aaron pull at his sleeve, saying, "do something!" I saw the water and the reeds, and I grabbed my timbrel, and I walked right in. The water felt alive from the moment I put my first sandal in. The Sea split when the water was right at my forehead.

Sometimes I think I might be more like Grandma Rebecca, whose decisive action made my family's story possible. Or like Grandma Sarah, who walked into foreign lands unafraid. But really, I'm just myself. The one who knew how to walk into deep water. My whole life, I always have.

Chag HaAviv
Environmental

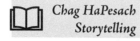
Chag HaPesach
Storytelling

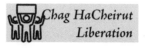
Chag HaCheirut
Liberation

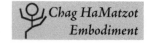
Chag HaMatzot
Embodiment

Hallel (Songs of Praise), Part I

Lift the cup of wine or grape juice and cover the matzah.

Therefore we must thank, praise, laud, glorify, exalt, lavish, bless, raise high, and acclaim God who made all these miracles for our ancestors and for us:

God brought us out from slavery to freedom, from sorrow to joy, from mourning to [celebration of] a festival, from darkness to great light, and from servitude to redemption.

And let us sing a new song— Halleluyah!

לְפִיכָךְ אֲנַחְנוּ חַיָּבִים לְהוֹדוֹת, לְהַלֵּל, לְשַׁבֵּחַ, לְפָאֵר, לְרוֹמֵם, לְהַדֵּר, לְבָרֵךְ, לְעַלֵּה וּלְקַלֵּס לְמִי שֶׁעָשָׂה לַאֲבוֹתֵינוּ וְלָנוּ אֶת־כָּל־ הַנִּסִּים הָאֵלּוּ: הוֹצִיאָנוּ מֵעַבְדוּת לְחֵרוּת מִיָּגוֹן לְשִׂמְחָה, וּמֵאֵבֶל לְיוֹם טוֹב, וּמֵאֲפֵלָה לְאוֹר גָּדוֹל, וּמִשִּׁעְבּוּד לִגְאֻלָּה. וְנֹאמַר לְפָנָיו שִׁירָה חֲדָשָׁה: הַלְלוּיָהּ.

When Israel's left from Egypt, the house of Jacob from a people of foreign speech. Yehudah became God's holy one; Israel, God's subjects. The Sea saw and fled; the River Jordan flowed backwards. The mountains danced like rams, the hills like lambs.

What is happening to you, O Sea, that you are fleeing, O Jordan that you flow backwards; O mountains that you dance like rams, O hills like lambs? From before the Master, dance O earth, from before the God of Jacob. God who turns the boulder into a pond of water, the flint into a spring of water. (Psalms 114)

בְּצֵאת יִשְׂרָאֵל מִמִּצְרָיִם, בֵּית יַעֲקֹב מֵעַם לֹעֵז, הָיְתָה יְהוּדָה לְקָדְשׁוֹ, יִשְׂרָאֵל מַמְשְׁלוֹתָיו. הַיָּם רָאָה וַיָּנֹס, הַיַּרְדֵּן יִסֹּב לְאָחוֹר. הֶהָרִים רָקְדוּ כְאֵילִים, גְּבָעוֹת כִּבְנֵי צֹאן.

מַה לְּךָ הַיָּם כִּי תָנוּס, הַיַּרְדֵּן - תִּסֹּב לְאָחוֹר, הֶהָרִים - תִּרְקְדוּ כְאֵילִים, גְּבָעוֹת כִּבְנֵי־צֹאן. מִלִּפְנֵי אָדוֹן חוּלִי אָרֶץ, מִלִּפְנֵי אֱלוֹהַ יַעֲקֹב. הַהֹפְכִי הַצּוּר אֲגַם־מָיִם, חַלָּמִישׁ לְמַעְיְנוֹ־מָיִם.

The Embodied Natural World

In Psalm 114, the natural world responds to the Exodus from Egypt with giddiness, joy, and glee. Can you envision how the natural world might embody a response to events today?

Chag HaAviv
Environmental

Chag HaPesach
Storytelling

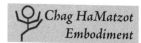
Chag HaCheirut
Liberation

Chag HaMatzot
Embodiment

Halleluyah! Praise, servants of God, praise the name of God. May the Name of the God be blessed from now and forever. From the rising of the sun in the East to its setting, the name of God is praised. Above all nations is the God, God's honor is above the heavens. Who is like our God, Who sits on high; Who looks down upon the heavens and the earth? God brings up the poor out of the dirt; God raises the destitute from the trash to seat them with the greats of God's people. God places a barren woman in a home, a happy mother of children. Halleluyah! (Psalms 113)

הַלְלוּיָהּ הַלְלוּ עַבְדֵי יהוה, הַלְלוּ אֶת־שֵׁם יהוה. יְהִי שֵׁם יהוה מְבֹרָךְ מֵעַתָּה וְעַד עוֹלָם. מִמִּזְרַח שֶׁמֶשׁ עַד מְבוֹאוֹ מְהֻלָּל שֵׁם יהוה. רָם עַל־כָּל־גּוֹיִם יהוה, עַל הַשָּׁמַיִם כְּבוֹדוֹ. מִי כַּיי אֱלֹהֵינוּ הַמַּגְבִּיהִי לָשָׁבֶת, הַמַּשְׁפִּילִי לִרְאוֹת בַּשָּׁמַיִם וּבָאָרֶץ? מְקִימִי מֵעָפָר דָּל, מֵאַשְׁפֹּת יָרִים אֶבְיוֹן, לְהוֹשִׁיבִי עִם־נְדִיבִים, עִם נְדִיבֵי עַמּוֹ. מוֹשִׁיבִי עֲקֶרֶת הַבַּיִת, אֵם הַבָּנִים שְׂמֵחָה. הַלְלוּיָהּ.

The Four Cups have many meanings. The second cup focuses on the four stages of life.

Second Cup: Stages Of Life

According to Rabbi Jacob Ettlinger (1798–1871, Prussia), each cup symbolizes a different stage of life. The first cup represents childhood, getting started. The second cup, as part of Maggid, represents youth and education. The third cup, concluding the meal, is connected to adulthood and providing food for one's family. The final cup, part of Hallel/praise, represents old age and gratitude.

Many queer thinkers, including J. Halberstam and Jules Ryan, have powerfully critiqued a straightforward model of "life stages" as heteronormative and in conflict with how queer people actually experience time.

Do you relate to having distinct life stages? Do they feel authentic or prescriptive to you? For the second cup, what is one aspect of your educational experience that felt particularly liberatory and you want to carry with you?

Second Cup

Lift the cup of wine or grape juice

בָּרוּךְ אַתָּה יהוה אֱלֹהֵינוּ מֶלֶךְ הָעוֹלָם, אֲשֶׁר גְּאָלָנוּ וְגָאַל אֶת־אֲבוֹתֵינוּ מִמִּצְרַיִם, וְהִגִּיעָנוּ הַלַּיְלָה הַזֶּה לֶאֱכָל־בּוֹ מַצָּה וּמָרוֹר. כֵּן יהוה אֱלֹהֵינוּ וֵאלֹהֵי אֲבוֹתֵינוּ יַגִּיעֵנוּ לְמוֹעֲדִים וְלִרְגָלִים אֲחֵרִים הַבָּאִים לִקְרָאתֵנוּ לְשָׁלוֹם, שְׂמֵחִים בְּבִנְיַן עִירֶךָ וְשָׂשִׂים בַּעֲבוֹדָתֶךָ. וְנֹאכַל שָׁם מִן הַזְּבָחִים וּמִן הַפְּסָחִים אֲשֶׁר יַגִּיעַ דָּמָם עַל קִיר מִזְבַּחֲךָ לְרָצוֹן, וְנוֹדֶה לְךָ שִׁיר חָדָשׁ עַל גְּאֻלָּתֵנוּ וְעַל פְּדוּת נַפְשֵׁנוּ. בָּרוּךְ אַתָּה יהוה, גָּאַל יִשְׂרָאֵל.

Blessed are You, Lord our God, Ruler of the universe, who redeemed us and redeemed our ancestors from Egypt, and brought us on this night to eat matzah and marror. Also, Lord our God, and God of our ancestors, bring us to other holidays and festivals in peace, joyful in the building of Your city and happy in Your worship. There we shall eat from the offerings and from the Pesach sacrifices, the blood of which shall reach the wall of Your altar for favor. We shall thank You with a new song upon our redemption and upon the restoration of our souls. Blessed are you, Lord, who redeems Israel.

Drink while reclining to the left

בָּרוּךְ אַתָּה יהוה, אֱלֹהֵינוּ מֶלֶךְ הָעוֹלָם בּוֹרֵא פְּרִי הַגָּפֶן.

Blessed are You, Lord our God, who creates the fruit of the vine.

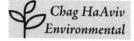 Chag HaAviv Environmental

 Chag HaPesach Storytelling

 Chag HaCheirut Liberation

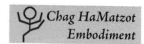 Chag HaMatzot Embodiment

The next several steps focus on some of the tangible and edible symbols of slavery and freedom. According to Rabban Gamliel, these are the crucial elements of the Seder.

רַבָּן גַּמְלִיאֵל הָיָה אוֹמֵר: כָּל שֶׁלֹּא
אָמַר שְׁלֹשָׁה דְּבָרִים אֵלּוּ בַּפֶּסַח,
לֹא יָצָא יְדֵי חוֹבָתוֹ, וְאֵלּוּ הֵן:

Rabban Gamliel used to say: Anyone who has not explained these three things on Pesach has not fulfilled their obligation, and they are:

פֶּסַח, מַצָּה, וּמָרוֹר.

the Pesach sacrifice, matzah, and marror.

Wash hands with the blessing. It is customary to link the handwashing to eating the matzah by avoiding speech or other distractions from the point of washing hands through eating the matzah.

בָּרוּךְ אַתָּה יהוה, אֱלֹהֵינוּ מֶלֶךְ הָעוֹלָם, אֲשֶׁר קִדְּשָׁנוּ בְּמִצְוֹתָיו וְצִוָּנוּ עַל
נְטִילַת יָדָיִם.

Blessed are You, Lord our God, Ruler of the Universe, who blessed us with commandments and obligated us to wash our hands.

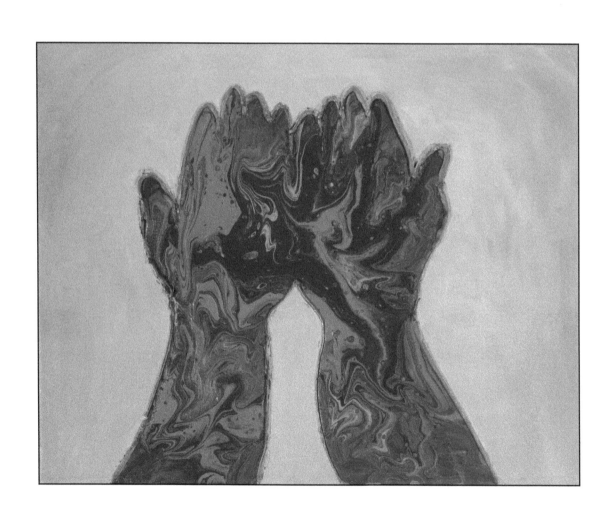

  Chag HaAviv
Environmental 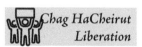 Chag HaPesach
Storytelling 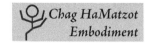 Chag HaCheirut
Liberation Chag HaMatzot
Embodiment

Matzah

מוֹצִיא מַצָּה

Lift and bless all three matzahs, keeping the broken one in the middle. After reciting the blessings, take a piece from the top matzah and from the broken middle matzah and eat them while reclining.

בָּרוּךְ אַתָּה יהוה, אֱלֹהֵינוּ מֶלֶךְ הָעוֹלָם הַמּוֹצִיא לֶחֶם מִן הָאָרֶץ.

Baruch Atah Adonai Eloheinu Melekh HaOlam hamotzi lechem min ha-aretz.

Blessed are You, Lord our God, Ruler of the Universe, who brings forth bread from the earth.

בָּרוּךְ אַתָּה יהוה, אֱלֹהֵינוּ מֶלֶךְ הָעוֹלָם, אֲשֶׁר קִדְּשָׁנוּ בְּמִצְוֹתָיו וְצִוָּנוּ עַל אֲכִילַת מַצָּה.

Baruch Atah Adonai Eloheinu Melekh HaOlam asher kidshanu b'mitzvotav v'tzivanu al achilat matzah.

Blessed are You, Lord our God, Ruler of the Universe, who blessed us with commandments and obligated us to eat the matzah.

Why are we eating this matzah, what is the reason? The reason is because our ancestors' dough was not yet able to rise, before they experienced the revelation of the Ruler of the rulers of rulers, the Holy Blessed One, who redeemed them, as it is stated (Exodus 12:39); "And they baked the dough which they brought out of Egypt into matzah cakes, since it did not rise; because they were expelled from Egypt, and could not tarry, neither had they made for themselves provisions."

מַצָּה זוֹ שֶׁאָנוּ אוֹכְלִים, עַל שׁוּם מָה? עַל שׁוּם שֶׁלֹּא הִסְפִּיק בְּצֵקָם שֶׁל אֲבוֹתֵינוּ לְהַחֲמִיץ עַד שֶׁנִּגְלָה עֲלֵיהֶם מֶלֶךְ מַלְכֵי הַמְּלָכִים, הַקָּדוֹשׁ בָּרוּךְ הוּא, וּגְאָלָם, שֶׁנֶּאֱמַר: וַיֹּאפוּ אֶת־הַבָּצֵק אֲשֶׁר הוֹצִיאוּ מִמִּצְרַיִם עֻגֹת מַצּוֹת, כִּי לֹא חָמֵץ, כִּי גֹרְשׁוּ מִמִּצְרַיִם וְלֹא יָכְלוּ לְהִתְמַהְמֵהַּ, וְגַם צֵדָה לֹא עָשׂוּ לָהֶם.

Maror

מָרוֹר

Take a piece of maror to eat without dipping.

Why are we eating this maror, what is the reason? The reason is because the Egyptians embittered the lives of our ancestors in Egypt, as it is stated (Exodus 1:14); "And they made their lives bitter with hard service, in mortar and in brick, and in all manner of service in the field; in all their service, wherein they made them serve in misery."

מָרוֹר זֶה שֶׁאָנוּ אוֹכְלִים, עַל שׁוּם מַה? עַל שׁוּם שֶׁמֵּרְרוּ הַמִּצְרִים אֶת־חַיֵּי אֲבוֹתֵינוּ בְּמִצְרָיִם, שֶׁנֶּאֱמַר: וַיְמָרְרוּ אֶת חַיֵּיהֶם בַּעֲבֹדָה קָשָׁה, בְּחֹמֶר וּבִלְבֵנִים וּבְכָל־עֲבֹדָה בַּשָּׂדֶה אֵת כָּל עֲבֹדָתָם אֲשֶׁר עָבְדוּ בָהֶם בְּפָרֶךְ.

בָּרוּךְ אַתָּה יהוה, אֱלֹהֵינוּ מֶלֶךְ הָעוֹלָם, אֲשֶׁר קִדְּשָׁנוּ בְּמִצְוֹתָיו וְצִוָּנוּ עַל אֲכִילַת מָרוֹר.

Baruch Atah Adonai Eloheinu Melekh HaOlam asher kidshanu b'mitzvotav v'tzivanu al achilat maror.

Blessed are You, Lord our God, Ruler of the Universe, who blessed us with commandments and obligated us to eat the maror.

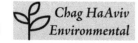 Chag HaAviv Environmental    Chag HaPesach Storytelling    Chag HaCheirut Liberation   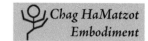 Chag HaMatzot Embodiment

Hillel Sandwich

בּוֹרֵךְ

Take from the bottom matzah and make a sandwich with the maror and charoset in the matzah.

Remember the Temple like Hillel. This is what Hillel would do when the Temple existed. He would wrap the matzah and marror and eat them together, to fulfill what is stated, (Exodus 12:15): "You should eat it with matzah and maror."

זֵכֶר לְמִקְדָּשׁ כְּהִלֵּל. כֵּן עָשָׂה הִלֵּל בִּזְמַן שֶׁבֵּית הַמִּקְדָּשׁ הָיָה קַיָּם. הָיָה כּוֹרֵךְ מַצָּה וּמָרוֹר וְאוֹכֵל בְּיַחַד, לְקַיֵּם מַה שֶׁנֶּאֱמַר: עַל מַצּוֹת וּמְרוֹרִים יֹאכְלֻהוּ.

The Passover sacrifice that our ancestors used to eat when the Temple existed, why did they eat it, what is the reason? The reason is to commemorate that the Holy Blessed One passed over the homes of our ancestors in Egypt, as it is stated (Exodus 12:27); "And you shall say: 'It is the passover sacrifice to the Lord, who passed over the homes of Bnei Yisrael in Egypt, when God smote the Egyptians, but our homes were saved.' And the people bowed the head and bowed."

פֶּסַח שֶׁהָיוּ אֲבוֹתֵינוּ אוֹכְלִים בִּזְמַן שֶׁבֵּית הַמִּקְדָּשׁ הָיָה קַיָּם, עַל שׁוּם מָה? עַל שׁוּם שֶׁפָּסַח הַקָּדוֹשׁ בָּרוּךְ הוּא עַל בָּתֵּי אֲבוֹתֵינוּ בְּמִצְרַיִם, שֶׁנֶּאֱמַר: וַאֲמַרְתֶּם זֶבַח פֶּסַח הוּא לַיָי, אֲשֶׁר פָּסַח עַל בָּתֵּי בְנֵי יִשְׂרָאֵל בְּמִצְרַיִם בְּנָגְפּוֹ אֶת־מִצְרַיִם, וְאֶת־בָּתֵּינוּ הִצִּיל וַיִּקֹּד הָעָם וַיִּשְׁתַּחֲווּ.

Dinner

שֻׁלְחָן עוֹרֵךְ

Enjoy dinner!

Seeing Love Tucked Into A Delicious Meal

The current was shifting. The water near shore changes direction first, followed by the deeper water midriver. I know this from paddling, how those currents near shore have unexpectedly pushed me the wrong direction. But knowing something is different from seeing something. I know there are currents, but I don't see them unless a stick is tossed in the water or ice dances north or south. It's like knowing the wind and seeing the wind, how it shuffles tree branches and raises dust. It's like knowing love and seeing love tucked into a delicious meal.
—Susan Fox Rogers, *My Reach*

 *Chag HaAviv*
Environmental

 *Chag HaPesach*
Storytelling

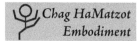 *Chag HaCheirut*
Liberation

Chag HaMatzot
Embodiment

Afikoman

The meal concludes with finding and eating the hidden half matzah from yachatz.

Hidden And Found, Forgotten And Remembered

There is a Jewish legend that when a potential child is still a drop in the womb, the angel Laila shows it all the mysteries of the world (Niddah 30b, Midrash Tanchuma Pekudei 3, etc.). When the baby is born, the angel comes back and slaps its face, causing it to forget everything from the womb lessons. (In some versions, the slap is a kiss or a caress, and it explains why we have the philtrum—the indentation between the nose and the upper lip.)

The story is reminiscent of Plato's philosophy of anamnesis. According to Plato, all learning is recollection. All humans posess internal knowledge. When we learn, it is not new. It is just remembering what we already understood.

As we find and eat the afikoman, consider: what knowledge do we know, but repeatedly forget? What do we hide from ourselves, just to find it later?

Bless

בָּרֵךְ:

Fill a cup with wine or grape juice for the third cup.

A Song of Ascents; When the Lord will bring back the captivity of Zion, we will be like dreamers. Then our mouth will be full of mirth and our tongue joyful melody; then they will say among the nations; "The Lord has done greatly with these." The Lord has done great things with us; we are happy. Lord, return our captivity like streams in the desert. Those that sow with tears will reap with joyful song. He who surely goes and cries, he carries the measure of seed, he will surely come in joyful song and carry his sheaves. (Psalms 126)

שִׁיר הַמַּעֲלוֹת, בְּשׁוּב יהוה אֶת שִׁיבַת צִיּוֹן הָיִינוּ כְּחֹלְמִים. אָז יִמָּלֵא שְׂחוֹק פִּינוּ וּלְשׁוֹנֵנוּ רִנָּה. אָז יֹאמְרוּ בַגּוֹיִם: הִגְדִּיל יהוה לַעֲשׂוֹת עִם אֵלֶּה. הִגְדִּיל יהוה לַעֲשׂוֹת עִמָּנוּ, הָיִינוּ שְׂמֵחִים. שׁוּבָה יהוה אֶת שְׁבִיתֵנוּ כַּאֲפִיקִים בַּנֶּגֶב. הַזֹּרְעִים בְּדִמְעָה, בְּרִנָּה יִקְצֹרוּ. הָלוֹךְ יֵלֵךְ וּבָכֹה נֹשֵׂא מֶשֶׁךְ הַזָּרַע, בֹּא יָבֹא בְרִנָּה נֹשֵׂא אֲלֻמֹּתָיו.

When more than three Jewish adults are present, include with the following invitation. Include the additions in brackets when ten or more Jewish adults are present.

Friends, let us bless.

חֲבֵרַי נְבָרֵךְ:   *Leader*

יְהִי שֵׁם יהוה מְבֹרָךְ מֵעַתָּה וְעַד עוֹלָם.   *Response, repeated by leader*

May the Name of the Lord be blessed from now and forever. (Psalms 113)

בִּרְשׁוּת רַבּוֹתַי, נְבָרֵךְ [אֱלֹהֵינוּ] שֶׁאָכַלְנוּ מִשֶּׁלּוֹ.   *Leader*

With your permission, let us bless [our God] whose food we have eaten.

בָּרוּךְ [אֱלֹהֵינוּ] שֶׁאָכַלְנוּ מִשֶּׁלּוֹ וּבְטוּבוֹ חָיִינוּ.   *Response, repeated by leader*

Bless [our God] whose food we have eaten and whose goodness enriches our lives.

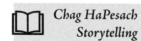
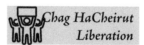

בָּרוּךְ אַתָּה יהוה, אֱלֹהֵינוּ מֶלֶךְ הָעוֹלָם, הַזָּן אֶת הָעוֹלָם כֻּלּוֹ בְּטוּבוֹ בְּחֵן בְּחֶסֶד וּבְרַחֲמִים, הוּא נוֹתֵן לֶחֶם לְכָל בָּשָׂר כִּי לְעוֹלָם חַסְדּוֹ. וּבְטוּבוֹ הַגָּדוֹל תָּמִיד לֹא חָסַר לָנוּ, וְאַל יֶחְסַר לָנוּ מָזוֹן לְעוֹלָם וָעֶד. בַּעֲבוּר שְׁמוֹ הַגָּדוֹל, כִּי הוּא אֵל זָן וּמְפַרְנֵס לַכֹּל וּמֵטִיב לַכֹּל, וּמֵכִין מָזוֹן לְכָל בְּרִיּוֹתָיו אֲשֶׁר בָּרָא. בָּרוּךְ אַתָּה יהוה, הַזָּן אֶת הַכֹּל.

Blessed are You, Lord our God, Ruler of the Universe, who nourishes the entire world in goodness, in grace, in kindness and in mercy. God gives bread to all flesh since God's kindness is forever. And in God's great goodness, we have never lacked, and may we not lack nourishment forever and always, because of His great name. Since God is a Power that feeds and provides for all and does good to all and prepares nourishment for all of God's creatures that God created. Blessed are You, Lord, who sustains all.

נוֹדֶה לְךָ יהוה אֱלֹהֵינוּ עַל שֶׁהִנְחַלְתָּ לַאֲבוֹתֵינוּ אֶרֶץ חֶמְדָּה טוֹבָה וּרְחָבָה, וְעַל שֶׁהוֹצֵאתָנוּ יהוה אֱלֹהֵינוּ מֵאֶרֶץ מִצְרַיִם, וּפְדִיתָנוּ מִבֵּית עֲבָדִים, וְעַל בְּרִיתְךָ שֶׁחָתַמְתָּ בִּבְשָׂרֵנוּ, וְעַל תּוֹרָתְךָ שֶׁלִּמַּדְתָּנוּ, וְעַל חֻקֶּיךָ שֶׁהוֹדַעְתָּנוּ, וְעַל חַיִּים חֵן וָחֶסֶד שֶׁחוֹנַנְתָּנוּ, וְעַל אֲכִילַת מָזוֹן שָׁאַתָּה זָן וּמְפַרְנֵס אוֹתָנוּ תָּמִיד, בְּכָל יוֹם וּבְכָל עֵת וּבְכָל שָׁעָה:
וְעַל הַכֹּל יהוה אֱלֹהֵינוּ, אֲנַחְנוּ מוֹדִים לָךְ וּמְבָרְכִים אוֹתָךְ, יִתְבָּרַךְ שִׁמְךָ בְּפִי כָּל חַי תָּמִיד לְעוֹלָם וָעֶד. כַּכָּתוּב: וְאָכַלְתָּ וְשָׂבָעְתָּ וּבֵרַכְתָּ אֶת יהוה אֱלֹהֶיךָ עַל הָאָרֶץ הַטֹּבָה אֲשֶׁר נָתַן לָךְ. בָּרוּךְ אַתָּה יהוה, עַל הָאָרֶץ וְעַל הַמָּזוֹן:

We thank you, Lord our God, that you have given as an inheritance to our ancestors a lovely, good and broad land, and that You took us out, Lord our God, from the land of Egypt and that You redeemed us from a house of slaves, and for Your covenant which You have sealed in our flesh, and for Your Torah that You have taught us, and for Your statutes which You have made known to us, and for life, grace and kindness that You have granted us and for the eating of nourishment that You feed and provide for us always, on all days, and at all times and in every hour.

And for everything, Lord our God, we thank You and bless You; may Your name be blessed by the mouth of all life, constantly forever and always, as it is written (Deuteronomy 8:10); "And you shall eat and you shall be satiated and you shall bless the Lord your God for the good land that God has given you." Blessed are You, Lord, for the land and for the nourishment.

Rice

It grew in the black mud.
It grew under the tiger's orange paws.
Its stems thicker than candles, and as straight.
Its leaves like the feathers of egrets, but green.
The grains cresting, wanting to burst.
Oh, blood of the tiger.

I don't want you to just sit at the table.
I don't want you just to eat, and be content.
I want you to walk into the fields
Where the water is shining, and the rice has risen.
I want you to stand there, far from the white tablecloth.
I want you to fill your hands with mud, like a blessing.

—Mary Oliver

רַחֶם נָא יהוה אֱלֹהֵינוּ עַל יִשְׂרָאֵל עַמֶּךָ וְעַל יְרוּשָׁלַיִם עִירֶךָ וְעַל צִיּוֹן מִשְׁכַּן
כְּבוֹדֶךָ וְעַל מַלְכוּת בֵּית דָּוִד מְשִׁיחֶךָ וְעַל הַבַּיִת הַגָּדוֹל וְהַקָּדוֹשׁ שֶׁנִּקְרָא
שִׁמְךָ עָלָיו: אֱלֹהֵינוּ אָבִינוּ, רְעֵנוּ זוּנֵנוּ פַּרְנְסֵנוּ וְכַלְכְּלֵנוּ וְהַרְוִיחֵנוּ, וְהַרְוַח
לָנוּ יהוה אֱלֹהֵינוּ מְהֵרָה מִכָּל צָרוֹתֵינוּ. וְנָא אַל תַּצְרִיכֵנוּ יהוה אֱלֹהֵינוּ, לֹא
לִידֵי מַתְּנַת בָּשָׂר וָדָם וְלֹא לִידֵי הַלְוָאָתָם, כִּי אִם לְיָדְךָ הַמְּלֵאָה הַפְּתוּחָה
הַקְּדוֹשָׁה וְהָרְחָבָה, שֶׁלֹּא נֵבוֹשׁ וְלֹא נִכָּלֵם לְעוֹלָם וָעֶד.

Please have mercy, Lord our God, upon Israel, Your people; and upon Jerusalem, Your city; and upon Zion, the dwelling place of Your Glory; and upon the monarchy of the House of David, Your appointed one; and upon the great and holy house that Your name is called upon. Our God, our Father, tend us, sustain us, provide for us, relieve us and give us quick relief, Lord our God, from all of our troubles. And please do not make us needy, Lord our God, not for the gifts of flesh and blood, and not for their loans, but rather from Your full, open, holy and broad hand, so that we not be embarrassed and we not be ashamed forever and always.

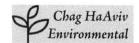 *Chag HaAviv* Environmental

 *Chag HaPesach* Storytelling

 *Chag HaCheirut* Liberation

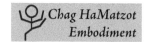 *Chag HaMatzot* Embodiment

May You be pleased to embolden us, Lord our God, in your commandments and in the command of the seventh day, of this great and holy Shabbat, since this day is great and holy before You, to cease work upon it and to rest upon it, with love, according to the commandment of Your will. And with Your will, allow us, Lord our God, that we should not have trouble, and grief and sighing on the day of our rest. And may You show us, Lord our God, the consolation of Zion, Your city; and the building of Jerusalem, Your holy city; since You are the Master of salvations and the Master of consolations.

רְצֵה וְהַחֲלִיצֵנוּ יהוה אֱלֹהֵינוּ בְּמִצְוֺתֶיךָ וּבְמִצְוַת יוֹם הַשְּׁבִיעִי הַשַּׁבָּת הַגָּדוֹל וְהַקָּדוֹשׁ הַזֶּה. כִּי יוֹם זֶה גָּדוֹל וְקָדוֹשׁ הוּא לְפָנֶיךָ לִשְׁבָּת בּוֹ וְלָנוּחַ בּוֹ בְּאַהֲבָה כְּמִצְוַת רְצוֹנֶךָ. וּבִרְצוֹנְךָ הָנִיחַ לָנוּ יהוה אֱלֹהֵינוּ שֶׁלֹּא תְהֵא צָרָה וְיָגוֹן וַאֲנָחָה בְּיוֹם מְנוּחָתֵנוּ. וְהַרְאֵנוּ יהוה אֱלֹהֵינוּ בְּנֶחָמַת צִיּוֹן עִירֶךָ וּבְבִנְיַן יְרוּשָׁלַיִם עִיר קָדְשֶׁךָ כִּי אַתָּה הוּא בַּעַל הַיְשׁוּעוֹת וּבַעַל הַנֶּחָמוֹת.

אֱלֹהֵינוּ וֵאלֹהֵי אֲבוֹתֵינוּ, יַעֲלֶה וְיָבֹא וְיַגִּיעַ וְיֵרָאֶה וְיֵרָצֶה וְיִשָּׁמַע וְיִפָּקֵד וְיִזָּכֵר זִכְרוֹנֵנוּ וּפִקְדוֹנֵנוּ, וְזִכְרוֹן אֲבוֹתֵינוּ, וְזִכְרוֹן מָשִׁיחַ בֶּן דָּוִד עַבְדֶּךָ, וְזִכְרוֹן יְרוּשָׁלַיִם עִיר קָדְשֶׁךָ, וְזִכְרוֹן כָּל עַמְּךָ בֵּית יִשְׂרָאֵל לְפָנֶיךָ, לִפְלֵיטָה לְטוֹבָה לְחֵן וּלְחֶסֶד וּלְרַחֲמִים, לְחַיִּים וּלְשָׁלוֹם בְּיוֹם חַג הַמַּצּוֹת הַזֶּה זָכְרֵנוּ יהוה אֱלֹהֵינוּ בּוֹ לְטוֹבָה וּפָקְדֵנוּ בּוֹ לִבְרָכָה וְהוֹשִׁיעֵנוּ בּוֹ לְחַיִּים. וּבִדְבַר יְשׁוּעָה וְרַחֲמִים חוּס וְחָנֵּנוּ וְרַחֵם עָלֵינוּ וְהוֹשִׁיעֵנוּ, כִּי אֵלֶיךָ עֵינֵינוּ, כִּי אֵל מֶלֶךְ חַנּוּן וְרַחוּם אָתָּה.

Please have mercy, Lord our God, upon Israel, Your people; and upon Jerusalem, Your city; and upon Zion, the dwelling place of Your Glory; and upon the monarchy of the House of David, Your appointed one; and upon the great and holy house that Your name is called upon. Our God, our Father, tend us, sustain us, provide for us, relieve us and give us quick relief, Lord our God, from all of our troubles. And please do not make us needy, Lord our God, not for the gifts of flesh and blood, and not for their loans, but rather from Your full, open, holy and broad hand, so that we not be embarrassed and we not be ashamed forever and always.

And may You build Jerusalem, the holy city, quickly and in our days. Blessed are You, Lord, who builds Jerusalem in Your mercy. Amen.

וּבְנֵה יְרוּשָׁלַיִם עִיר הַקֹּדֶשׁ בִּמְהֵרָה בְיָמֵינוּ. בָּרוּךְ אַתָּה יהוה, בּוֹנֵה בְרַחֲמָיו יְרוּשָׁלָיִם. אָמֵן.

בָּרוּךְ אַתָּה יהוה, אֱלֹהֵינוּ מֶלֶךְ הָעוֹלָם, הָאֵל אָבִינוּ מַלְכֵּנוּ אַדִּירֵנוּ בּוֹרְאֵנוּ גּוֹאֲלֵנוּ יוֹצְרֵנוּ קְדוֹשֵׁנוּ קְדוֹשׁ יַעֲקֹב רוֹעֵנוּ רוֹעֵה יִשְׂרָאֵל הַמֶּלֶךְ הַטּוֹב וְהַמֵּטִיב לַכֹּל שֶׁבְּכָל יוֹם וָיוֹם הוּא הֵטִיב, הוּא מֵטִיב, הוּא יֵיטִיב לָנוּ. הוּא גְמָלָנוּ הוּא גוֹמְלֵנוּ הוּא יִגְמְלֵנוּ לָעַד, לְחֵן וּלְחֶסֶד וּלְרַחֲמִים וּלְרֶוַח הַצָּלָה וְהַצְלָחָה, בְּרָכָה וִישׁוּעָה נֶחָמָה פַרְנָסָה וְכַלְכָּלָה וְרַחֲמִים וְחַיִּים וְשָׁלוֹם וְכָל טוֹב, וּמִכָּל טוּב לְעוֹלָם עַל יְחַסְּרֵנוּ.

Blessed are You, Lord our God, Ruler of the Universe, the Power, our Parent, our Ruler, our Mighty One, our Creator, our Redeemer, our Shaper, our Holy One, the Holy One of Jacob, our Shepherd, the Shepherd of Israel, the good Ruler, who does good to all, since on every single day God has done good, does good, and will do good, to us. God has granted us, grants us, and will grant us forever — in grace and in kindness, and in mercy, and in relief — rescue and success, blessing and salvation, consolation, provision and relief and mercy and life and peace and all good; and may we not lack any good ever.

 Chag HaAviv *Environmental*

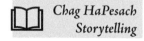 Chag HaPesach *Storytelling*

 Chag HaCheirut *Liberation*

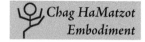 Chag HaMatzot *Embodiment*

May the Compassionate One reign over us forever and always.

May the Compassionate One be blessed in the heavens and in the earth.

May the Compassionate One be praised for all generations, and exalted among us forever and ever, and glorified among us always and infinitely for all infinities.

May the Compassionate One sustain us honorably.

May the Compassionate One break the yoke from upon our necks and bring us upright to our land.

May the Compassionate One send us multiple blessing, to this home and upon this table upon which we have eaten.

May the Compassionate One send us Eliyahu the prophet — may he be remembered for good — and he shall announce to us tidings of good, of salvation and of consolation.

הָרַחֲמָן הוּא יִמְלוֹךְ עָלֵינוּ לְעוֹלָם וָעֶד.

הָרַחֲמָן הוּא יִתְבָּרֵךְ בַּשָּׁמַיִם וּבָאָרֶץ.

הָרַחֲמָן הוּא יִשְׁתַּבַּח לְדוֹר דּוֹרִים, וְיִתְפָּאַר בָּנוּ לָעַד וּלְנֵצַח נְצָחִים, וְיִתְהַדַּר בָּנוּ לָעַד וּלְעוֹלְמֵי עוֹלָמִים.

הָרַחֲמָן הוּא יְפַרְנְסֵנוּ בְּכָבוֹד.

הָרַחֲמָן הוּא יִשְׁבּוֹר עֻלֵּנוּ מֵעַל צַוָּארֵנוּ, וְהוּא יוֹלִיכֵנוּ קוֹמְמִיּוּת לְאַרְצֵנוּ.

הָרַחֲמָן הוּא יִשְׁלַח לָנוּ בְּרָכָה מְרֻבָּה בַּבַּיִת הַזֶּה, וְעַל שֻׁלְחָן זֶה שֶׁאָכַלְנוּ עָלָיו.

הָרַחֲמָן הוּא יִשְׁלַח לָנוּ אֶת אֵלִיָּהוּ הַנָּבִיא זָכוּר לַטּוֹב, וִיבַשֶּׂר לָנוּ בְּשׂוֹרוֹת טוֹבוֹת יְשׁוּעוֹת וְנֶחָמוֹת.

May the Compassionate One bless each and every one of those here (especially those honored…), their families, the seeds they carry, and all that is theirs… (and also bless) us and all that is ours, just as our ancestral mothers Sarah, Rebecca, Rachel and Bilhah, Leah and Zilpah were [each] blessed: well (*Genesis 12:16*), goodly (24:16), better (29:19), good (30:20)

And as our ancestral fathers, Abraham, Isaac, and Jacob, [were each blessed]: in everything (Genesis 24:1), from everything (27:33), with everything (33:11), so too should God bless us all as one with a perfect blessing and we shall say, Amen.

May the merit of our ancestors advocate in Heaven on our behalf and bring us a lasting peace on Earth. And may we be blessed from the Lord and held accountable from the God of our salvation; and find kindness in the eyes of God and humanity.

הָרַחֲמָן הוּא יְבָרֵךְ אֶת....וְאֶת כָּל בַמְסֻבִּין כָּאן, אוֹתָם וְאֶת בֵּיתָם וְאֶת זַרְעָם וְאֶת כָּל אֲשֶׁר לָהֶם... אוֹתָנוּ וְאֶת כָּל אֲשֶׁר לָנוּ,

כְּמוֹ שֶׁנִּתְבָּרְכוּ אִמּוֹתֵינוּ שָׂרָה רִבְקָה רָחֵל וּבִלְהָה, לֵיאָה וְזִלְפָּה, הֵיטִיב, טָבַת, טוֹב, טוֹב.

וַאֲבוֹתֵינוּ אַבְרָהָם יִצְחָק וְיַעֲקֹב בַּכֹּל מִכֹּל כֹּל, כֵּן יְבָרֵךְ אוֹתָנוּ כֻּלָנוּ יַחַד בִּבְרָכָה שְׁלֵמָה, וְנֹאמַר, אָמֵן. בַמָּרוֹם יְלַמְּדוּ עֲלֵיהֶם וְעָלֵינוּ זְכוּת שֶׁתְּהֵא לְמִשְׁמֶרֶת שָׁלוֹם. וְנִשָּׂא בְרָכָה מֵאֵת יהוה, וּצְדָקָה מֵאֱלֹהֵי יִשְׁעֵנוּ, וְנִמְצָא חֵן וְשֵׂכֶל טוֹב בְּעֵינֵי אֱלֹהִים וְאָדָם.

On Shabbat add:

May the Compassionate One give us to inherit the day that will be completely Shabbat and rest in everlasting life.

On Shabbat, add:

הָרַחֲמָן הוּא יַנְחִילֵנוּ יוֹם שֶׁכֻּלוֹ שַׁבָּת וּמְנוּחָה לְחַיֵּי הָעוֹלָמִים.

May the Compassionate One allow us to inherit the day that will be all good. [The day that is all long, the day that the righteous will sit with their crowns on their heads enjoying the radiance of the Divine presence and may our share be with them.]

הָרַחֲמָן הוּא יַנְחִילֵנוּ יוֹם שֶׁכֻּלוֹ טוֹב.[יוֹם שֶׁכֻּלוֹ אָרוּךְ. יוֹם שֶׁצַּדִּיקִים יוֹשְׁבִים וְעַטְרוֹתֵיהֶם בְּרָאשֵׁיהֶם וְנֶהֱנִים מִזִּיו הַשְּׁכִינָה וִיהִי חֶלְקֵנוּ עִמָּהֶם.]

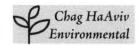
Chag HaAviv
Environmental

Chag HaPesach
Storytelling

Chag HaCheirut
Liberation

Chag HaMatzot
Embodiment

May the Compassionate One give us merit for the times of the messiah and for life in the world to come.

A tower of salvations is our Ruler; may God do kindness with the messiah, with David and his offspring, forever (II Samuel 22:51). The One who makes peace above, may He make peace upon us and upon all of Israel; and say, Amen.

Fear the Lord, God's holy ones, since there is no lacking for those that fear God. Young lions may go without and hunger, but those that seek the Lord will not lack any good thing (Psalms 34:10-11). Thank the Lord, since God is good, since God kindness is forever (Psalms 118:1). You open Your hand and satisfy the will of all living things (Psalms 146:16). Blessed is the person who trusts in the Lord and the Lord is their security (Jeremiah 17:7). I was a youth and I have also aged and I have not seen a righteous person forsaken and their offspring seeking bread (Psalms 37:25). The Lord will give courage to God's people. The Lord will bless God's people with peace (Psalms 29:11).

הָרַחֲמָן הוּא יְזַכֵּנוּ לִימוֹת הַמָּשִׁיחַ וּלְחַיֵּי הָעוֹלָם הַבָּא.
מִגְדּוֹל יְשׁוּעוֹת מַלְכּוֹ וְעֹשֶׂה חֶסֶד לִמְשִׁיחוֹ לְדָוִד וּלְזַרְעוֹ עַד עוֹלָם.
עֹשֶׂה שָׁלוֹם בִּמְרוֹמָיו, הוּא יַעֲשֶׂה שָׁלוֹם עָלֵינוּ וְעַל כָּל יִשְׂרָאֵל וְאִמְרוּ, אָמֵן.
יְראוּ אֶת יהוה קְדֹשָׁיו, כִּי אֵין מַחְסוֹר לִירֵאָיו. כְּפִירִים רָשׁוּ וְרָעֵבוּ, וְדֹרְשֵׁי יהוה לֹא יַחְסְרוּ כָל טוֹב. הוֹדוּ לַיהוה כִּי טוֹב כִּי לְעוֹלָם חַסְדּוֹ. פּוֹתֵחַ אֶת יָדֶךָ, וּמַשְׂבִּיעַ לְכָל חַי רָצוֹן. בָּרוּךְ הַגֶּבֶר אֲשֶׁר יִבְטַח בַּיהוה, וְהָיָה יהוה מִבְטַחוֹ. נַעַר הָיִיתִי גַּם זָקַנְתִּי, וְלֹא רָאִיתִי צַדִּיק נֶעֱזָב, וְזַרְעוֹ מְבַקֶּשׁ לָחֶם. יהוה עֹז לְעַמּוֹ יִתֵּן, יהוה יְבָרֵךְ אֶת עַמּוֹ בַשָּׁלוֹם.

The Four Cups have many meanings. The third cup focuses on the four mothers.

Third Cup: Mothers

Rabbi Isaiah Horowitz (1555–1630, Prague) taught that the four cups correspond to the four mothers.

Sarah connects to the first cup. In the kiddush we acknowledge that God chose us among the peoples. Sarah, one of the first two Jews by choice, chose God.

Rebecca is the cup of telling the story. She was there at the very beginning of the rupture in the family and sent Jacob to Lavan.

In the third cup, we honor Rachel. The third cup leads into the *shfoch chamatcha*, the moment of strong righteous anger. Rachel fights for what should be her inheritance when she steals the household idols.

Leah is the fourth cup of joy and gratitude. She praises God with gratitude when she births her children.

Which of the mothers do you most relate to?
How do you tell their stories?
Who are the people who mother you?
Who do you mother?
What will your legacy be?

Drink while reclining to the left   בָּרוּךְ אַתָּה יהוה, אֱלֹהֵינוּ מֶלֶךְ הָעוֹלָם בּוֹרֵא פְּרִי הַגָּפֶן.

Blessed are You, Lord our God, who creates the fruit of the vine.

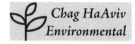 Chag HaAviv Environmental

 Chag HaPesach Storytelling

 Chag HaCheirut Liberation

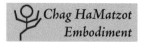 Chag HaMatzot Embodiment

Shfoch Chamatcha/Pour Out Your Wrath

Some fill Elijah's cup here, and some wait until after this passage is recited.
Either way, pick up Elijah's cup, stand in body and/or spirit, and open the door to outside.

Pour your wrath upon the nations that did not know You and upon the kingdoms that did not call upon Your Name! Since they have consumed Jacob and laid waste his habitation (Psalms 79:6-7). Pour out Your fury upon them and the fierceness of Your anger shall reach them (Psalms 69:25)! You shall pursue them with anger and eradicate them from under the skies of the Lord (Eicha 3:66).

שְׁפֹךְ חֲמָתְךָ אֶל־הַגּוֹיִם אֲשֶׁר לֹא יְדָעוּךָ וְעַל־מַמְלָכוֹת אֲשֶׁר בְּשִׁמְךָ לֹא קָרָאוּ. כִּי אָכַל אֶת־יַעֲקֹב וְאֶת־נָוֵהוּ הֵשַׁמּוּ. שְׁפָךְ־עֲלֵיהֶם זַעְמֶךָ וַחֲרוֹן אַפְּךָ יַשִּׂיגֵם. תִּרְדֹּף בְּאַף וְתַשְׁמִידֵם מִתַּחַת שְׁמֵי יְהוָה.

Leil Shimurim

Seder night has been referred to as "Leil Shimurim," a night that is guarded. The best seders are nights of vulnerability: discussing oppression, redemption, and freedom. But for much of Jewish history, seder nights were vulnerable for another reason: they were historically a night of pogroms and antisemitic violence. Most of the seder celebrates the move from slavery to freedom and from oppression to redemption. In *shfoch chamatcha*, we take a moment to think about how broken the world still is and to express our pain and our powerlessness.

Anger Is A Wonderful Useful Emotion

I think anger is a wonderful useful emotion and nothing to be ashamed of. It took me a long time to come to that, to make it constructively useful rather than just an outlet. The coming of HIV allowed all that. I don't know why I am the way I am but I'm glad of it.

—Larry Kramer

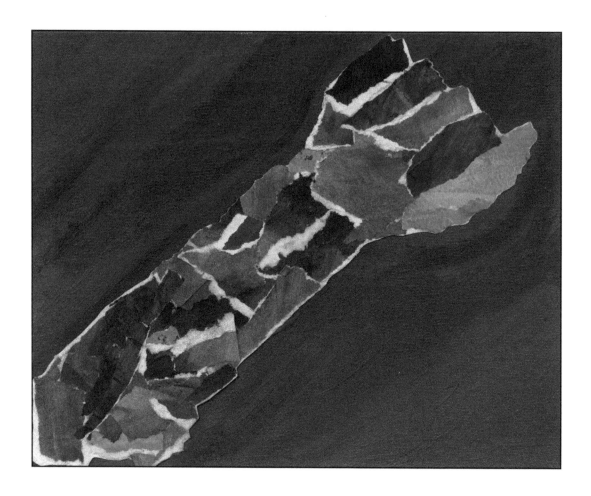

Built Doomed In The First Place

Some worlds are built on a fault line of pain, held up by nightmares. Don't lament when those worlds fall. Rage that they were built doomed in the first place.

—N.K. Jemisin, *The Stone Sky*

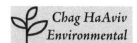 *Chag HaAviv* Environmental

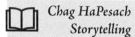 *Chag HaPesach* Storytelling

 *Chag HaCheirut* Liberation

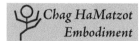 *Chag HaMatzot* Embodiment

Elijah is known as the harbinger of the messianic age. Pass around Elijah's cup so each participant can pour a portion of their wine or grape juice into it to symbolize how they contribute to building a more just world.

אֵלִיָּהוּ הַנָּבִיא, אֵלִיָּהוּ הַתִּשְׁבִּי, אֵלִיָּהוּ הַגִּלְעָדִי.
בִּמְהֵרָה בְיָמֵינוּ יָבוֹא אֵלֵינוּ, עִם מָשִׁיחַ בֶּן דָּוִד

Eliyahu hanavi, Eliyahu hatishbi, Eliyahu hagiladi.
Bimheirah biyameinu yavoh eleinu im Mashiach ben David.

Our Part In Bringing Redemption

We are all part of bringing redemption. How will you bring the lessons from the seder to fight against today's Pharaohs and ensure more freedom and liberation for all?

Imagine The Angels Of Bread

This is the year that squatters evict landlords,
gazing like admirals from the rail
of the roofdeck
or levitating hands in praise
of steam in the shower;
this is the year
that shawled refugees deport judges,
who stare at the floor
and their swollen feet
as files are stamped
with their destination;
this is the year that police revolvers,
stove-hot, blister the fingers
of raging cops,
and nightsticks splinter
in their palms;
this is the year
that darkskinned men
lynched a century ago
return to sip coffee quietly
with the apologizing descendants
of their executioners.
This is the year that those
who swim the border's undertow
and shiver in boxcars
are greeted with trumpets and drums
at the first railroad crossing
on the other side;
this is the year that the hands
pulling tomatoes from the vine
uproot the deed to the earth that sprouts
the vine,
the hands canning tomatoes

are named in the will
that owns the bedlam of the cannery;
this is the year that the eyes
stinging from the poison that purifies toilets
awaken at last to the sight
of a rooster-loud hillside,
pilgrimage of immigrant birth;
this is the year that cockroaches
become extinct, that no doctor
finds a roach embedded
in the ear of an infant;
this is the year that the food stamps
of adolescent mothers
are auctioned like gold doubloons,
and no coin is given to buy machetes
for the next bouquet of severed heads
in coffee plantation country.
If the abolition of slave-manacles
began as a vision of hands without manacles,
then this is the year;
if the shutdown of extermination camps
began as imagination of a land
without barbed wire or the crematorium,
then this is the year;
if every rebellion begins with the idea
that conquerors on horseback
are not many-legged gods, that they too
drown
if plunged in the river,
then this is the year.
So may every humiliated mouth,
teeth like desecrated headstones,
fill with the angels of bread.

—Martin Espada

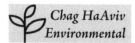 Chag HaAviv
Environmental

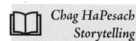 Chag HaPesach
Storytelling

 Chag HaCheirut
Liberation

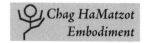 Chag HaMatzot
Embodiment

Hallel

הַלֵּל

Pour the fourth cup.

Not to us, not to us, but rather to Your name, give glory for your kindness and for your truth. Why should the nations say, "Say, where is their God?" But our God is in the heavens. All that God wanted, God has done. Their idols are silver and gold, the work of human hands. They have a mouth but do not speak; they have eyes but do not see. They have ears but do not hear; they have a nose but do not smell. Hands, but they do not feel; feet, but do not walk; they do not make a peep from their throat. Like them will be their makers, all those that trust in them.

Israel, trust in the Lord; their help and shield is God. House of Aharon, trust in the Lord; their help and shield is God. Those that fear the Lord, trust in the Lord; their help and shield is God.

לֹא לָנוּ, יהוה, לֹא לָנוּ, כִּי לְשִׁמְךָ תֵּן כָּבוֹד, עַל חַסְדְּךָ עַל אֲמִתֶּךָ. לָמָּה יֹאמְרוּ הַגּוֹיִם אַיֵּה נָא אֱלֹהֵיהֶם. וֵאלֹהֵינוּ בַשָּׁמָיִם, כֹּל אֲשֶׁר חָפֵץ עָשָׂה. עֲצַבֵּיהֶם כֶּסֶף וְזָהָב מַעֲשֵׂה יְדֵי אָדָם. פֶּה לָהֶם וְלֹא יְדַבֵּרוּ, עֵינַיִם לָהֶם וְלֹא יִרְאוּ. אָזְנַיִם לָהֶם וְלֹא יִשְׁמָעוּ, אַף לָהֶם וְלֹא יְרִיחוּן. יְדֵיהֶם וְלֹא יְמִישׁוּן, רַגְלֵיהֶם וְלֹא יְהַלֵּכוּ, לֹא יֶהְגּוּ בִּגְרוֹנָם. כְּמוֹהֶם יִהְיוּ עֹשֵׂיהֶם, כֹּל אֲשֶׁר בֹּטֵחַ בָּהֶם.
יִשְׂרָאֵל בְּטַח בַּיי, עֶזְרָם וּמָגִנָּם הוּא. בֵּית אַהֲרֹן בִּטְחוּ בַיי, עֶזְרָם וּמָגִנָּם הוּא. יִרְאֵי ה' בִּטְחוּ בַיי, עֶזְרָם וּמָגִנָּם הוּא.

יי זְכָרָנוּ יְבָרֵךְ. יְבָרֵךְ אֶת בֵּית יִשְׂרָאֵל, יְבָרֵךְ אֶת בֵּית אַהֲרֹן, יְבָרֵךְ יִרְאֵי יְהוָה, הַקְּטַנִּים עִם הַגְּדֹלִים. יֹסֵף יְהוָה עֲלֵיכֶם, עֲלֵיכֶם וְעַל בְּנֵיכֶם. בְּרוּכִים אַתֶּם לַיי, עֹשֵׂה שָׁמַיִם וָאָרֶץ. הַשָּׁמַיִם שָׁמַיִם לַיי וְהָאָרֶץ נָתַן לִבְנֵי אָדָם. לֹא הַמֵּתִים יְהַלְלוּ יָהּ וְלֹא כָּל יֹרְדֵי דוּמָה. וַאֲנַחְנוּ נְבָרֵךְ יָהּ מֵעַתָּה וְעַד עוֹלָם. הַלְלוּיָהּ.

The Lord who remembers us, will bless; God will bless the House of Israel; God will bless the House of Aharon. God will bless those that fear the Lord, the small ones with the great ones. May the Lord bring increase to you, to you and to your children. Blessed are you to the Lord, the maker of the heavens and the earth. The heavens, are the Lord's heavens, but the earth God has given to humanity. It is not the dead that will praise the Lord, and not those that go down to silence. But we will bless the Lord from now and forever. Halleluyah!

(Psalms 115)

אָהַבְתִּי כִּי יִשְׁמַע יְהוָה אֶת קוֹלִי תַּחֲנוּנָי. כִּי הִטָּה אָזְנוֹ לִי וּבְיָמַי אֶקְרָא. אֲפָפוּנִי חֶבְלֵי מָוֶת וּמְצָרֵי שְׁאוֹל מְצָאוּנִי, צָרָה וְיָגוֹן אֶמְצָא. וּבְשֵׁם יְהוָה אֶקְרָא: אָנָּא יְהוָה מַלְּטָה נַפְשִׁי. חַנּוּן יְהוָה וְצַדִּיק, וֵאלֹהֵינוּ מְרַחֵם. שֹׁמֵר פְּתָאִים יְהוָה, דַּלּוֹתִי וְלִי יְהוֹשִׁיעַ. שׁוּבִי נַפְשִׁי לִמְנוּחָיְכִי, כִּי יְהוָה גָּמַל עָלָיְכִי. כִּי חִלַּצְתָּ נַפְשִׁי מִמָּוֶת, אֶת עֵינִי מִן דִּמְעָה, אֶת רַגְלִי מִדֶּחִי. אֶתְהַלֵּךְ לִפְנֵי יְהוָה בְּאַרְצוֹת הַחַיִּים. הֶאֱמַנְתִּי כִּי אֲדַבֵּר, אֲנִי עָנִיתִי מְאֹד. אֲנִי אָמַרְתִּי בְחָפְזִי כָּל הָאָדָם כֹּזֵב.

I have loved the Lord — since God hears my voice, my supplications. Since God inclined God's ear to me — and in my days, I will call out. The pangs of death have encircled me and the straits of the Pit have found me and I found grief. And in the name of the Lord I called, "Please Lord, Spare my soul." Gracious is the Lord and righteous, and our God acts mercifully. The Lord watches over the silly; I was poor and God has saved me. Return, my soul to your tranquility, since the Lord has favored you. Since You have rescued my soul from death, my eyes from tears, my feet from stumbling. I will walk before the Lord in the lands of the living. I have trusted, when I speak — I am very afflicted. I said in my haste, all people are hypocritical.

(Psalms 116:1-11)

 Chag HaAviv Environmental

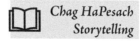 Chag HaPesach Storytelling

 Chag HaCheirut Liberation

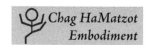 Chag HaMatzot Embodiment

מָה אָשִׁיב לַיי כָּל תַּגְמוּלוֹהִי עָלָי. כּוֹס יְשׁוּעוֹת אֶשָּׂא וּבְשֵׁם יהוה אֶקְרָא. נְדָרַי לַיי אֲשַׁלֵּם נֶגְדָה נָּא לְכָל עַמּוֹ. יָקָר בְּעֵינֵי יהוה הַמָּוְתָה לַחֲסִידָיו. אָנָּה יהוה כִּי אֲנִי עַבְדֶּךָ, אֲנִי עַבְדְּךָ בֶּן אֲמָתֶךָ, פִּתַּחְתָּ לְמוֹסֵרָי. לְךָ אֶזְבַּח זֶבַח תּוֹדָה וּבְשֵׁם יהוה אֶקְרָא. נְדָרַי לַיי אֲשַׁלֵּם נֶגְדָה נָּא לְכָל עַמּוֹ. בְּחַצְרוֹת בֵּית יהוה, בְּתוֹכֵכִי יְרוּשָׁלָיִם. הַלְלוּיָהּ.

What can I give back to the Lord for all that God has favored me? A cup of salvations I will raise up and I will call out in the name of the Lord. My vows to the Lord I will pay, now in front of God's entire people. Precious in the eyes of the Lord is the death of God's pious ones. Please Lord, since I am Your servant, the son of Your maidservant; You have opened my chains. To You will I offer a thanksgiving offering and I will call out in the name of the Lord. My vows to the Lord I will pay, now in front of God's entire people. In the courtyards of the house of the Lord, in your midst, Jerusalem. Halleluyah!

(Psalms 116:12-19)

הַלְלוּ אֶת יהוה כָּל גּוֹיִם, שַׁבְּחוּהוּ כָּל הָאֻמִּים. כִּי גָבַר עָלֵינוּ חַסְדּוֹ, וֶאֱמֶת יהוה לְעוֹלָם. הַלְלוּיָהּ. הוֹדוּ לַיי כִּי טוֹב כִּי לְעוֹלָם חַסְדּוֹ. יֹאמַר נָא יִשְׂרָאֵל כִּי לְעוֹלָם חַסְדּוֹ. יֹאמְרוּ נָא בֵית אַהֲרֹן כִּי לְעוֹלָם חַסְדּוֹ. יֹאמְרוּ נָא יִרְאֵי יהוה כִּי לְעוֹלָם חַסְדּוֹ.

Praise the name of the Lord, all nations; extol God all peoples. Since God's kindness has overwhelmed us and the truth of the Lord is forever. Halleluyah! Thank the Lord, since God is good, since God's kindness is forever. Let Israel now say, "Thank the Lord, since God is good, since God's kindness is forever." Let the House of Aharon now say, "Thank the Lord, since God is good, since God's kindness is forever." Let those that fear the Lord now say, "Thank the Lord, since God is good, since God's kindness is forever."

(Psalms 117-118:4)

מִן הַמֵּצַר קָרָאתִי יָה, עָנָנִי בַמֶּרְחַב יָה.

יְהוה לִי, לֹא אִירָא - מַה יַּעֲשֶׂה לִי אָדָם, יְהוה לִי בְּעֹזְרָי וַאֲנִי אֶרְאֶה בְּשֹׂנְאָי. טוֹב לַחֲסוֹת בַּיי מִבְּטֹחַ בָּאָדָם. טוֹב לַחֲסוֹת בַּיי מִבְּטֹחַ בִּנְדִיבִים. כָּל גּוֹיִם סְבָבוּנִי, בְּשֵׁם יהוה כִּי אֲמִילַם. סַבּוּנִי גַם סְבָבוּנִי, בְּשֵׁם יהוה כִּי אֲמִילַם. סַבּוּנִי כִדְבֹרִים, דֹּעֲכוּ כְּאֵשׁ קוֹצִים, בְּשֵׁם יהוה כִּי אֲמִילַם. דָּחֹה דְחִיתַנִי לִנְפֹּל, וַיי עֲזָרָנִי. עָזִּי וְזִמְרָת יָה וַיְהִי לִי לִישׁוּעָה. קוֹל רִנָּה וִישׁוּעָה בְּאָהֳלֵי צַדִּיקִים: יְמִין ה' עֹשָׂה חָיִל, יְמִין ה' רוֹמֵמָה, יְמִין ה' עֹשָׂה חָיִל. לֹא אָמוּת כִּי אֶחְיֶה, וַאֲסַפֵּר מַעֲשֵׂי יָה. יַסֹּר יִסְּרַנִי יָּה, וְלַמָּוֶת לֹא נְתָנָנִי.

From the narrowness I have called, Lord; God answered me from the wide abundance. The Lord is for me, I will not fear, what will people do to me? The Lord is for me with my helpers, and I shall glare at those that hate me. It is better to take refuge with the Lord than to trust in humanity. It is better to take refuge with the Lord than to trust in nobles. All the nations surrounded me — in the name of the Lord, as I will chop them off. They surrounded me, they also encircled me — in the name of the Lord, as I will chop them off. They surrounded me like bees, they were extinguished like a fire of thorns — in the name of the Lord, as I will chop them off. You have surely pushed me to fall, but the Lord helped me. My strength and song is the Lord, and God has become my salvation. The sound of happy song and salvation is in the tents of the righteous, the right hand of the Lord acts powerfully. I will not die but rather I will live and tell over the acts of the Lord. The Lord has surely chastised me, but God has not given me over to death.

(Psalms 118:5-18)

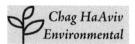 *Chag HaAviv* Environmental

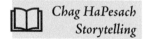 *Chag HaPesach* Storytelling

 *Chag HaCheirut* Liberation

 *Chag HaMatzot* Embodiment

פִּתְחוּ לִי שַׁעֲרֵי צֶדֶק, אָבֹא בָם, אוֹדֶה יָהּ.

זֶה הַשַּׁעַר לַיְיָ, צַדִּיקִים יָבֹאוּ בוֹ.

אוֹדְךָ כִּי עֲנִיתָנִי וַתְּהִי לִי לִישׁוּעָה.

אֶבֶן מָאֲסוּ הַבּוֹנִים הָיְתָה לְרֹאשׁ פִּנָּה.

מֵאֵת יהוה הָיְתָה זֹּאת הִיא נִפְלָאת בְּעֵינֵינוּ.

זֶה הַיּוֹם עָשָׂה יהוה. נָגִילָה וְנִשְׂמְחָה בוֹ.

Open up for me the gates of righteousness; I will enter them, thank the Lord.
This is the gate of the Lord, the righteous will enter it.
I will thank You, since You answered me and You have become my salvation.
The stone that was left by the builders has become the main cornerstone.
From the Lord was this, it is wondrous in our eyes.
This is the day of the Lord, let us exult and rejoice upon it.

(Psalms 118:19-24)

Please, Lord, save us now!
Please, Lord, help us succeed now!
(Psalms 118:25)

אָנָּא יהוה, הוֹשִׁיעָה נָּא.

אָנָּא יהוה, הוֹשִׁיעָה נָּא.

אָנָּא יהוה, הַצְלִיחָה נָּא.

אָנָּא יהוה, הַצְלִיחָה נָּא.

Hallel   94

Blessed be the one who comes in the name of the Lord, we have blessed you from the house of the Lord. God is the Lord, and has illuminated us. Tie up the festival offering with ropes until it reaches the corners of the altar. You are my Power and I will Thank You; my God and I will exalt You. Thank the Lord, since God is good, since God's kindness is forever.

(Psalms 118:26-29)

בָּרוּךְ הַבָּא בְּשֵׁם יהוה, בֵּרַכְנוּכֶם מִבֵּית יהוה.
אֵל יהוה וַיָּאֶר לָנוּ. אִסְרוּ חַג בַּעֲבֹתִים עַד קַרְנוֹת הַמִּזְבֵּחַ.
אֵלִי אַתָּה וְאוֹדֶךָּ, אֱלֹהַי - אֲרוֹמְמֶךָּ.
הוֹדוּ לַיי כִּי טוֹב, כִּי לְעוֹלָם חַסְדּוֹ.

All of your works shall praise You, Lord our God, and your pious ones, the righteous ones who do Your will; and all of Your people, the House of Israel will thank and bless in joyful song: and extol and glorify, and exalt and acclaim, and sanctify and coronate Your name, our Ruler. Since, You it is good to thank, and to Your name it is pleasant to sing, since from always and forever are you the Power.

יְהַלְלוּךָ יהוה אֱלֹהֵינוּ כָּל מַעֲשֶׂיךָ, וַחֲסִידֶיךָ צַדִּיקִים עוֹשֵׂי רְצוֹנֶךָ, וְכָל עַמְּךָ בֵּית יִשְׂרָאֵל בְּרִנָּה יוֹדוּ וִיבָרְכוּ, וִישַׁבְּחוּ וִיפָאֲרוּ, וִירוֹמְמוּ וְיַעֲרִיצוּ, וְיַקְדִּישׁוּ וְיַמְלִיכוּ אֶת שְׁמָךְ, מַלְכֵּנוּ. כִּי לְךָ טוֹב לְהוֹדוֹת וּלְשִׁמְךָ נָאֶה לְזַמֵּר, כִּי מֵעוֹלָם וְעַד עוֹלָם אַתָּה אֵל.

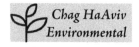 Chag HaAviv Environmental

 Chag HaPesach Storytelling

 Chag HaCheirut Liberation

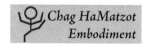 Chag HaMatzot Embodiment

כִּי לְעוֹלָם חַסְדּוֹ.	הוֹדוּ לַיהוה כִּי טוֹב
כִּי לְעוֹלָם חַסְדּוֹ.	הוֹדוּ לֵאלֹהֵי הָאֱלֹהִים
כִּי לְעוֹלָם חַסְדּוֹ.	הוֹדוּ לַאֲדֹנֵי הָאֲדֹנִים
כִּי לְעוֹלָם חַסְדּוֹ.	לְעֹשֵׂה נִפְלָאוֹת גְּדֹלוֹת לְבַדּוֹ
כִּי לְעוֹלָם חַסְדּוֹ.	לְעֹשֵׂה הַשָּׁמַיִם בִּתְבוּנָה
כִּי לְעוֹלָם חַסְדּוֹ.	לְרוֹקַע הָאָרֶץ עַל הַמָּיִם
כִּי לְעוֹלָם חַסְדּוֹ.	לְעֹשֵׂה אוֹרִים גְּדֹלִים
כִּי לְעוֹלָם חַסְדּוֹ.	אֶת הַשֶּׁמֶשׁ לְמֶמְשֶׁלֶת בַּיּוֹם
	אֶת הַיָּרֵחַ וְכוֹכָבִים
כִּי לְעוֹלָם חַסְדּוֹ.	לְמֶמְשְׁלוֹת בַּלָּיְלָה
כִּי לְעוֹלָם חַסְדּוֹ.	לְמַכֵּה מִצְרַיִם בִּבְכוֹרֵיהֶם
כִּי לְעוֹלָם חַסְדּוֹ.	וַיּוֹצֵא יִשְׂרָאֵל מִתּוֹכָם
כִּי לְעוֹלָם חַסְדּוֹ.	בְּיָד חֲזָקָה וּבִזְרוֹעַ נְטוּיָה
כִּי לְעוֹלָם חַסְדּוֹ.	לְגֹזֵר יַם סוּף לִגְזָרִים
כִּי לְעוֹלָם חַסְדּוֹ.	וְהֶעֱבִיר יִשְׂרָאֵל בְּתוֹכוֹ
כִּי לְעוֹלָם חַסְדּוֹ.	וְנִעֵר פַּרְעֹה וְחֵילוֹ בְיַם סוּף
כִּי לְעוֹלָם חַסְדּוֹ.	לְמוֹלִיךְ עַמּוֹ בַּמִּדְבָּר
כִּי לְעוֹלָם חַסְדּוֹ.	לְמַכֵּה מְלָכִים גְּדֹלִים
כִּי לְעוֹלָם חַסְדּוֹ.	וַיַּהֲרֹג מְלָכִים אַדִּירִים
כִּי לְעוֹלָם חַסְדּוֹ.	לְסִיחוֹן מֶלֶךְ הָאֱמֹרִי
כִּי לְעוֹלָם חַסְדּוֹ.	וּלְעוֹג מֶלֶךְ הַבָּשָׁן
כִּי לְעוֹלָם חַסְדּוֹ.	וְנָתַן אַרְצָם לְנַחֲלָה
כִּי לְעוֹלָם חַסְדּוֹ.	נַחֲלָה לְיִשְׂרָאֵל עַבְדּוֹ
כִּי לְעוֹלָם חַסְדּוֹ.	שֶׁבְּשִׁפְלֵנוּ זָכַר לָנוּ
כִּי לְעוֹלָם חַסְדּוֹ.	וַיִּפְרְקֵנוּ מִצָּרֵינוּ
כִּי לְעוֹלָם חַסְדּוֹ.	נֹתֵן לֶחֶם לְכָל בָּשָׂר
כִּי לְעוֹלָם חַסְדּוֹ.	הוֹדוּ לְאֵל הַשָּׁמָיִם

Thank the Lord, since God is good, since God's kindness is forever.
Thank the Power of powers.
To the Master of masters.
To the One who alone does wondrously great deeds.
To the one who made the Heavens with discernment.
To the One who spread the earth over the waters.
To the One who made great lights.
The sun to rule in the day.
The moon and the stars to rule in the night.
To the One that smote Egypt through their firstborn.
And God took Israel out from among them.
With a strong hand and an outstretched forearm.
To the One who cut up the Reed Sea into strips.
And made Israel to pass through it.
And jolted Pharaoh and his troop in the Reed Sea.
To the One who led God's people in the wilderness.
To the One who smote great kings.
And killed mighty kings.
Sichon, king of the Amorite.
And Og, king of the Bashan.
And God gave their land as an inheritance.
An inheritance for Israel, God's servant.
That in our lowliness, God remembered us.
And God delivered us from our adversaries.
God gives bread to all flesh.
Thank the Power of the heavens, since God's kindness is forever.

(Psalms 136)

 *Chag HaAviv*
Environmental

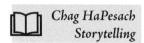 *Chag HaPesach*
Storytelling

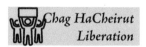 *Chag HaCheirut*
Liberation

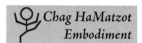 *Chag HaMatzot*
Embodiment

The Interconnectedness of All Living Beings

The word neshama refers to soul and is closely linked to breath and spirit. Nishmat kol chai [the soul of all living beings] is often understood as referring to land animals. However, plants—from trees to phytoplankton—make breath possible. When we read "nishmat kol chai," we remember the plants that photosynthesize and respirate; the fungi that break down decaying matter so the nutrients can be recycled; the mangroves, coral, oysters, and grasses that protect our coasts; and the interconnectedness of all living beings.

The soul of every living being shall bless Your Name, Lord our God; the spirit of all flesh shall glorify and exalt Your remembrance always, our Leader. From the world and until the world, You are the Power, and other than You we have no ruler, redeemer, or savior, restorer, rescuer, provider, and compassionate one in every time of distress and anguish; we have no ruler, besides You! God of the first ones and the last ones, God of all creatures, Master of all Generations, Who is praised through a multitude of praises, Who guides the world with kindness and the creatures with mercy. The Lord neither slumbers nor sleeps. God who rouses the sleepers and awakens the dozers; God who makes the mute speak, and frees the captives, and supports the falling, and straightens the bent. We thank You alone.

נִשְׁמַת כָּל חַי תְּבָרֵךְ אֶת שִׁמְךָ, יְהֹוָה אֱלֹהֵינוּ, וְרוּחַ כָּל בָּשָׂר תְּפָאֵר וּתְרוֹמֵם זִכְרְךָ, מַלְכֵּנוּ, תָּמִיד. מִן הָעוֹלָם וְעַד הָעוֹלָם אַתָּה אֵל, וּמִבַּלְעָדֶיךָ אֵין לָנוּ מֶלֶךְ גּוֹאֵל וּמוֹשִׁיעַ, פּוֹדֶה וּמַצִּיל וּמְפַרְנֵס וּמְרַחֵם בְּכָל עֵת צָרָה וְצוּקָה. אֵין לָנוּ מֶלֶךְ אֶלָּא אַתָּה. אֱלֹהֵי הָרִאשׁוֹנִים וְהָאַחֲרוֹנִים, אֱלוֹהַּ כָּל בְּרִיּוֹת, אֲדוֹן כָּל תּוֹלָדוֹת, הַמְהֻלָּל בְּרֹב הַתִּשְׁבָּחוֹת, הַמְנַהֵג עוֹלָמוֹ בְּחֶסֶד וּבְרִיּוֹתָיו בְּרַחֲמִים. וַיהֹוָה לֹא יָנוּם וְלֹא יִישָׁן - הַמְעוֹרֵר יְשֵׁנִים וְהַמֵּקִיץ נִרְדָּמִים, וְהַמֵּשִׂיחַ אִלְּמִים וְהַמַּתִּיר אֲסוּרִים וְהַסּוֹמֵךְ נוֹפְלִים וְהַזּוֹקֵף כְּפוּפִים. לְךָ לְבַדְּךָ אֲנַחְנוּ מוֹדִים.

 Chag HaAviv
Environmental

 Chag HaPesach
Storytelling

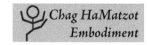 Chag HaCheirut
Liberation

Chag HaMatzot
Embodiment

Were our mouth as full of song as the sea, and our tongue as full of joyous song as its multitude of waves, and our lips as full of praise as the breadth of the heavens, and our eyes as sparkling as the sun and the moon, and our hands as outspread as the eagles of the sky and our feet as swift as deers — we still could not thank You sufficiently, Lord our God and God of our ancestors, and to bless Your Name for one thousandth of the thousand of thousands of thousands, and myriad myriads, of goodnesses that You performed for our ancestors and for us. From Egypt, Lord our God, did you redeem us and from the house of slaves you restored us. In famine You nourished us, and in plenty you sustained us. From the sword you saved us, and from plague you spared us; and from severe and enduring diseases you delivered us.

Until now Your mercy has helped us, and Your kindness has not forsaken us; and do not abandon us, Lord our God, forever. Therefore, the limbs that You set within us and the spirit and soul that You breathed into our nostrils, and the tongue that You placed in our mouth — verily, they shall thank and bless and praise and glorify, and exalt and revere, and sanctify and coronate Your name, our Ruler.

אִלּוּ פִינוּ מָלֵא שִׁירָה כַּיָּם, וּלְשׁוֹנֵנוּ רִנָּה כַּהֲמוֹן גַּלָּיו, וְשִׂפְתוֹתֵינוּ שֶׁבַח כְּמֶרְחֲבֵי רָקִיעַ, וְעֵינֵינוּ מְאִירוֹת כַּשֶּׁמֶשׁ וְכַיָּרֵחַ, וְיָדֵינוּ פְרוּשׂוֹת כְּנִשְׁרֵי שָׁמָיִם, וְרַגְלֵינוּ קַלּוֹת כָּאַיָּלוֹת — אֵין אֲנַחְנוּ מַסְפִּיקִים לְהוֹדוֹת לְךָ, יהוה אֱלֹהֵינוּ וֵאלֹהֵי אֲבוֹתֵינוּ, וּלְבָרֵךְ אֶת שְׁמֶךָ עַל אַחַת מֵאֶלֶף, אַלְפֵי אֲלָפִים וְרִבֵּי רְבָבוֹת פְּעָמִים הַטּוֹבוֹת שֶׁעָשִׂיתָ עִם אֲבוֹתֵינוּ וְעִמָּנוּ. מִמִּצְרַיִם גְּאַלְתָּנוּ, יהוה אֱלֹהֵינוּ, וּמִבֵּית עֲבָדִים פְּדִיתָנוּ, בְּרָעָב זַנְתָּנוּ וּבְשָׂבָע כִּלְכַּלְתָּנוּ, מֵחֶרֶב הִצַּלְתָּנוּ וּמִדֶּבֶר מִלַּטְתָּנוּ, וּמֵחֳלָיִם רָעִים וְנֶאֱמָנִים דִּלִּיתָנוּ.

עַד הֵנָּה עֲזָרוּנוּ רַחֲמֶיךָ וְלֹא עֲזָבוּנוּ חֲסָדֶיךָ, וְאַל תִּטְּשֵׁנוּ, יהוה אֱלֹהֵינוּ, לָנֶצַח. עַל כֵּן אֵבָרִים שֶׁפִּלַּגְתָּ בָּנוּ וְרוּחַ וּנְשָׁמָה שֶׁנָּפַחְתָּ בְּאַפֵּינוּ וְלָשׁוֹן אֲשֶׁר שַׂמְתָּ בְּפִינוּ — הֵן הֵם יוֹדוּ וִיבָרְכוּ וִישַׁבְּחוּ וִיפָאֲרוּ וִירוֹמְמוּ וְיַעֲרִיצוּ וְיַקְדִּישׁוּ וְיַמְלִיכוּ אֶת שִׁמְךָ מַלְכֵּנוּ.

The Full Impact of its Unimaginable Beauty and Wonder

What would it mean for a soul that truly captured it; this life in which the emphasis should lie on the immediate percepts, the messages the world pours in on us, instead of on the sophisticated universe into which our clever brains transmute them? ...It would mean that we should receive from every flower, not merely a beautiful image to which the label "flower" has been fixed, but the full impact of its unimaginable beauty and wonder, the direct sensation of life having communion with life: that the scents of the ceasing rain, the voice of the trees, the deep softness of the kitten's fur, the acrid touch of sorrel on the tongue, should be in themselves profound, complete, and simple experiences, calling forth simplicity of response in our souls.
—Evelyn Underhill, *Practical Mysticism: A Little Book for Normal People*

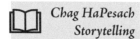
Chag HaAviv
Environmental

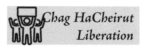
Chag HaPesach
Storytelling

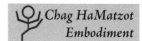
Chag HaCheirut
Liberation

Chag HaMatzot
Embodiment

For every mouth shall offer thanks to You; and every tongue shall swear allegiance to You; and every knee shall bend to You; and every upright one shall prostrate themselves before You; all hearts shall fear You; and all innermost feelings and thoughts shall sing praises to Your name, as the matter is written (Psalms 35:10), "All my bones shall say, 'Lord, who is like You? You save the poor man from one who is stronger than he, the poor and destitute from the one who would rob him.'"

Who is similar to You and who is equal to You and who can be compared to You, O great, strong and awesome Power, O highest Power, Creator of the heavens and the earth. We shall praise and extol and glorify and bless Your holy name, as it is stated (Psalms 103:1), " [A Psalm] of David. Bless the Lord, O my soul; and all that is within me, God's holy name." The Power, in Your powerful boldness; the Great, in the glory of Your name; the Strong One forever; the Ruler who sits on the high and elevated throne. God who dwells

כִּי כָל פֶּה לְךָ יוֹדֶה, וְכָל לָשׁוֹן לְךָ תִּשָּׁבַע, וְכָל בֶּרֶךְ לְךָ תִכְרַע, וְכָל קוֹמָה לְפָנֶיךָ תִשְׁתַּחֲוֶה, וְכָל לְבָבוֹת יִירָאוּךָ, וְכָל קֶרֶב וּכְלָיוֹת יְזַמְּרוּ לִשְׁמֶךָ. כַּדָּבָר שֶׁכָּתוּב, כָּל עַצְמוֹתַי תֹּאמַרְנָה, יהוה מִי כָמוֹךָ מַצִּיל עָנִי מֵחָזָק מִמֶּנּוּ וְעָנִי וְאֶבְיוֹן מִגֹּזְלוֹ. מִי יִדְמֶה לָּךְ וּמִי יִשְׁוֶה לָּךְ וּמִי יַעֲרָךְ לָךְ הָאֵל הַגָּדוֹל, הַגִּבּוֹר וְהַנּוֹרָא, אֵל עֶלְיוֹן, קֹנֵה שָׁמַיִם וָאָרֶץ. נְהַלֶּלְךָ וּנְשַׁבֵּחֲךָ וּנְפָאֶרְךָ וּנְבָרֵךְ אֶת שֵׁם קָדְשֶׁךָ, כָּאָמוּר: לְדָוִד, בָּרְכִי נַפְשִׁי אֶת יהוה וְכָל קְרָבַי אֶת שֵׁם קָדְשׁוֹ. הָאֵל בְּתַעֲצֻמוֹת עֻזֶּךָ, הַגָּדוֹל בִּכְבוֹד שְׁמֶךָ, הַגִּבּוֹר לָנֶצַח וְהַנּוֹרָא בְּנוֹרְאוֹתֶיךָ, הַמֶּלֶךְ הַיּוֹשֵׁב עַל כִּסֵּא רָם וְנִשָּׂא. שׁוֹכֵן עַד מָרוֹם וְקָדוֹשׁ שְׁמוֹ. וְכָתוּב: רַנְּנוּ צַדִּיקִים בַּיהוה, לַיְשָׁרִים נָאוָה תְהִלָּה. בְּפִי יְשָׁרִים תִּתְהַלָּל, וּבְדִבְרֵי צַדִּיקִים תִּתְבָּרַךְ, וּבִלְשׁוֹן חֲסִידִים תִּתְרוֹמָם, וּבְקֶרֶב קְדוֹשִׁים תִּתְקַדָּשׁ.

always; lofty and holy is God's name. And as it is written (Psalms 33:10), "Sing joyfully to the Lord, righteous ones, praise is beautiful from the upright." By the mouth of the upright You shall be praised; By the lips of the righteous shall You be blessed; By the tongue of the devout shall You be exalted; And among the holy shall You be sanctified.

And in the assemblies of the myriads of Your people Israel, in joyous song will Your name be glorified, our Leader, in each and every generation. It is the duty of all creatures, before You, Lord our God, and God of our ancestors, to thank, to praise, to extol, to glorify, to exalt, to lavish, to bless, to raise high and to acclaim — beyond the words of the songs and praises of David, the son of Yishai, Your servant, Your anointed one.

May Your name be praised forever, our Ruler, the Power, the Great and holy Ruler — in the heavens and in the earth. Since for You it is pleasant — O Lord our God and God of our ancestors — song and lauding, praise and hymn, boldness and dominion, triumph, greatness and strength, psalm and splendor, holiness and kingship, blessings and thanksgivings, from now and forever. Blessed are You Lord, Power, Ruler exalted through laudings, Power of thanksgivings, Master of Wonders, who chooses the songs of hymn — Ruler, Power of the life of the worlds.

וּבְמַקְהֲלוֹת רִבְבוֹת עַמְּךָ בֵּית יִשְׂרָאֵל בְּרִנָּה יִתְפָּאֵר שִׁמְךָ, מַלְכֵּנוּ, בְּכָל דּוֹר וָדוֹר, שֶׁכֵּן חוֹבַת כָּל הַיְצוּרִים לְפָנֶיךָ, יהוה אֱלֹהֵינוּ וֵאלֹהֵי אֲבוֹתֵינוּ, לְהוֹדוֹת לְהַלֵּל לְשַׁבֵּחַ, לְפָאֵר לְרוֹמֵם לְהַדֵּר לְבָרֵךְ, לְעַלֵּה וּלְקַלֵּס עַל כָּל דִּבְרֵי שִׁירוֹת וְתִשְׁבְּחוֹת דָּוִד בֶּן יִשַׁי עַבְדְּךָ מְשִׁיחֶךָ.

יִשְׁתַּבַּח שִׁמְךָ לָעַד מַלְכֵּנוּ, הָאֵל הַמֶּלֶךְ הַגָּדוֹל וְהַקָּדוֹשׁ בַּשָּׁמַיִם וּבָאָרֶץ, כִּי לְךָ נָאֶה, יהוה אֱלֹהֵינוּ וֵאלֹהֵי אֲבוֹתֵינוּ, שִׁיר וּשְׁבָחָה, הַלֵּל וְזִמְרָה, עֹז וּמֶמְשָׁלָה, נֶצַח, גְּדֻלָּה וּגְבוּרָה, תְּהִלָּה וְתִפְאֶרֶת, קְדֻשָּׁה וּמַלְכוּת, בְּרָכוֹת וְהוֹדָאוֹת מֵעַתָּה וְעַד עוֹלָם. בָּרוּךְ אַתָּה יהוה, אֵל מֶלֶךְ גָּדוֹל בַּתִּשְׁבָּחוֹת, אֵל הַהוֹדָאוֹת, אֲדוֹן הַנִּפְלָאוֹת, הַבּוֹחֵר בְּשִׁירֵי זִמְרָה, מֶלֶךְ אֵל חֵי הָעוֹלָמִים.

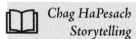
Chag HaAviv
Environmental

Chag HaPesach
Storytelling

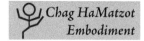
Chag HaCheirut
Liberation

Chag HaMatzot
Embodiment

Fourth Cup

Drink while reclining to the left

בָּרוּךְ אַתָּה יהוה, אֱלֹהֵינוּ מֶלֶךְ הָעוֹלָם בּוֹרֵא פְּרִי הַגָּפֶן.

Blessed are You, Lord our God, who creates the fruit of the vine.

בָּרוּךְ אַתָּה יהוה אֱלֹהֵינוּ מֶלֶךְ הָעוֹלָם, עַל הַגֶּפֶן וְעַל פְּרִי הַגֶּפֶן, עַל
תְּנוּבַת הַשָּׂדֶה וְעַל אֶרֶץ חֶמְדָּה טוֹבָה וּרְחָבָה שֶׁרָצִיתָ וְהִנְחַלְתָּ לַאֲבוֹתֵינוּ
לֶאֱכוֹל מִפִּרְיָהּ וְלִשְׂבּוֹעַ מִטּוּבָהּ. רַחֵם נָא ה' אֱלֹהֵינוּ עַל יִשְׂרָאֵל עַמֶּךָ וְעַל
יְרוּשָׁלַיִם עִירֶךָ וְעַל צִיּוֹן מִשְׁכַּן כְּבוֹדֶךָ וְעַל מִזְבְּחֶךָ וְעַל הֵיכָלֶךָ וּבְנֵה
יְרוּשָׁלַיִם עִיר הַקֹּדֶשׁ בִּמְהֵרָה בְיָמֵינוּ וְהַעֲלֵנוּ לְתוֹכָהּ וְשַׂמְּחֵנוּ בְּבִנְיָנָהּ
וְנֹאכַל מִפִּרְיָהּ וְנִשְׂבַּע מִטּוּבָהּ וּנְבָרֶכְךָ עָלֶיהָ בִּקְדֻשָּׁה וּבְטָהֳרָה [בשבת:
וּרְצֵה וְהַחֲלִיצֵנוּ בְּיוֹם הַשַּׁבָּת הַזֶּה] וְשַׂמְּחֵנוּ בְּיוֹם חַג הַמַּצּוֹת הַזֶּה, כִּי
אַתָּה ה' טוֹב וּמֵטִיב לַכֹּל, וְנוֹדֶה לְּךָ עַל הָאָרֶץ וְעַל פְּרִי הַגָּפֶן. בָּרוּךְ אַתָּה
יהוה, עַל הָאָרֶץ וְעַל פְּרִי הַגָּפֶן.

Blessed are You, Lord our God, Ruler of the universe, for the vine and for the fruit of the vine; and for the bounty of the field; and for a desirable, good and broad land, which You wanted to give to our fathers, to eat from its fruit and to be satiated from its goodness. Please have mercy, Lord our God upon Israel Your people; and upon Jerusalem, Your city: and upon Zion, the dwelling place of Your glory; and upon Your altar; and upon Your sanctuary; and build Jerusalem Your holy city quickly in our days, and bring us up into it and gladden us in its building; and we shall eat from its fruit, and be satiated from its goodness, and bless You in holiness and purity. [On Shabbat: And may you be pleased to embolden us on this Shabbat day] and gladden us on this day of the Festival of Matzot. Since You, Lord, are good and do good to all, we thank You for the land and for the fruit of the vine. Blessed are You, Lord, for the land and for the fruit of the vine.

The Four Cups have many meanings. The fourth cup focuses on types of freedom.

Fourth Cup: Different Kinds Of Freedom

Rabbi Yochanan teaches each of the four cups correspond to a different freedom found in Exodus 6:6-7:

"וְהוֹצֵאתִי," "וְהִצַּלְתִּי," "וְגָאַלְתִּי," "וְלָקַחְתִּי"

"I will bring you out"; "I will rescue you"; "I will redeem you"; "I will take you"

—Jerusalem Talmud Pesachim 68b

In the Torah Temimah commentary (p. 1904), Rabbi Baruch Halevi Epstein teaches that these are not different words for the same freedom, but rather different kinds of freedom.

Do you agree? Where do you see the distinction? For this final cup of wine, where do you want this year to take you?

Sensual Vitality Is Essential

Sensual vitality is essential to the struggle for life. Many people drink as if filling themselves with dirt or starch: the filling of emptiness. But what comes after is a greater emptiness... But there's a sensual vitality in drinking wine and "spirits" as in drinking pure water. Both belong to ancient human rites and memories. People have fermented the apple, the grape, the palm, hops and barley, rice, berries, the potato, the dandelion, the plum. Along with the rising of the yeast in bread was the fermentation of the grain, the fruit. Blessed be the Spirit of the Universe, who created the fruit of the vine. For us to use as we may.

—Adrienne Rich, *What is Found There*

Chag HaAviv
Environmental

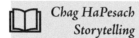
Chag HaPesach
Storytelling

Chag HaCheirut
Liberation

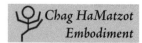
Chag HaMatzot
Embodiment

Conclusion नְרְצָה

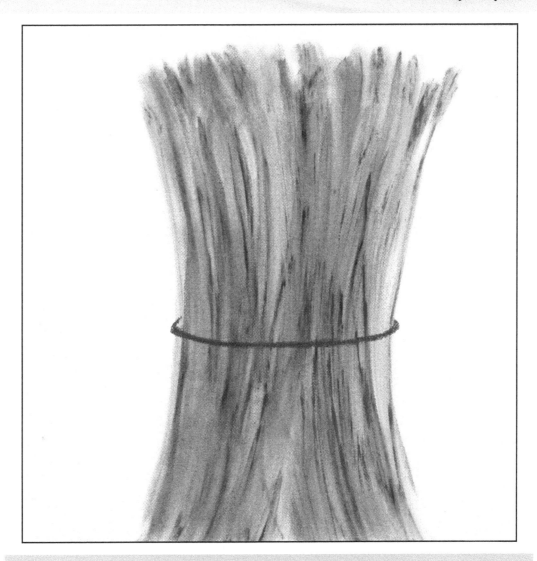

Counting The Days Of The Harvest

We count the omer between Passover and Shavuot to remember the barley harvest. The omer itself refers to the unit of barley sheaves. Israelites also harvested their first fruits of the year during this time.

   In many climates outside the Mediterranean, Passover falls at the very beginning of spring, before much is ready to be harvested at all. What is growing where you live? What would you like to nurture and grow over the next seven weeks?

Counting the Omer

On the second night of Passover, count the omer.
On the first night of Passover, skip this page.

We now complete the Arami Oved Avi statement that was started and explicated in Maggid. In Deuteronomy, this formula was recited when each pilgrim brought their fruits to the Temple to contribute. The portion in Maggid stops short of completing the passage, so we finish it here, to bridge the communal history and mythology to present abundance and gratitude.

וַיְבִאֵנוּ אֶל־הַמָּקוֹם הַזֶּה וַיִּתֶּן־לָנוּ אֶת־הָאָרֶץ הַזֹּאת אֶרֶץ זָבַת חָלָב וּדְבָשׁ. וְעַתָּה הִנֵּה הֵבֵאתִי אֶת־רֵאשִׁית פְּרִי הָאֲדָמָה אֲשֶׁר־נָתַתָּה לִי יהוה.

God brought us to this place and gave us this land, a land flowing with milk and honey. So I now bring the first fruits of the soil which You, O Lord, have given me.

בָּרוּךְ אַתָּה יהוה, אֱלֹהֵינוּ מֶלֶךְ הָעוֹלָם, אֲשֶׁר קִדְּשָׁנוּ בְּמִצְוֹתָיו וְצִוָּנוּ עַל סְפִירַת הָעֹמֶר.
הַיּוֹם יוֹם אֶחָד בָּעֹמֶר.

Blessed are You, Lord our God, Ruler of the Universe, who has sanctified us with commandments and has commanded us on the counting of the omer.
Today is the first day of the omer.

Counting The Days From Oppression To Justice

We count the omer between Passover and Shavuot to symbolize the time between leaving Egypt and receiving the Torah. We move from slavery and oppression to a society defined by a shared commitment to justice and holiness.
How can you bring more justice into your life over the next seven weeks?

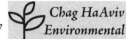 *Chag HaAviv* Environmental

 *Chag HaPesach* Storytelling

 *Chag HaCheirut* Liberation

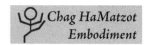 *Chag HaMatzot* Embodiment

Who Knows One?

Echad mi yodeah? Echad ani yodeah. Echad Eloheinu, Eloheinu, Eloheinu, Eloheinu shebashamayim u'ba'aretz.

Who knows one? I know one. One is our God, one is is our God, one is our God—in the heavens and the earth.

Who knows two? I know two. Two are the tablets that Moshe brought.

Who knows three? I know three. Three are the papas.

Who knows four? I know four. Four are the mamas.

Who knows five? I know five. Five are the books of the Torah.

Who knows six? I know six. Six are the books of the Mishnah.

Who knows seven? I know seven. Seven are the days of the week.

Who knows eight? I know eight. Eight are the days until brit milah.

Who knows nine? I know nine. Nine are the months of pregnancy.

אֶחָד מִי יוֹדֵעַ?

אֶחָד מִי יוֹדֵעַ? אֶחָד אֲנִי יוֹדֵעַ: אֶחָד אֱלֹהֵינוּ שֶׁבַּשָּׁמַיִם וּבָאָרֶץ.

שְׁנַיִם מִי יוֹדֵעַ? שְׁנַיִם אֲנִי יוֹדֵעַ: שְׁנֵי לֻחוֹת הַבְּרִית. אֶחָד אֱלֹהֵינוּ שֶׁבַּשָּׁמַיִם וּבָאָרֶץ.

שְׁלֹשָׁה מִי יוֹדֵעַ? שְׁלֹשָׁה אֲנִי יוֹדֵעַ: שְׁלֹשָׁה אָבוֹת, שְׁנֵי לֻחוֹת הַבְּרִית, אֶחָד אֱלֹהֵינוּ שֶׁבַּשָּׁמַיִם וּבָאָרֶץ.

אַרְבַּע מִי יוֹדֵעַ? אַרְבַּע אֲנִי יוֹדֵעַ: אַרְבַּע אִמָּהוֹת, שְׁלֹשָׁה אָבוֹת, שְׁנֵי לֻחוֹת הַבְּרִית, אֶחָד אֱלֹהֵינוּ שֶׁבַּשָּׁמַיִם וּבָאָרֶץ.

חֲמִשָּׁה מִי יוֹדֵעַ? חֲמִשָּׁה אֲנִי יוֹדֵעַ: חֲמִשָּׁה חוּמְשֵׁי תוֹרָה, אַרְבַּע אִמָּהוֹת, שְׁלֹשָׁה אָבוֹת, שְׁנֵי לֻחוֹת הַבְּרִית, אֶחָד אֱלֹהֵינוּ שֶׁבַּשָּׁמַיִם וּבָאָרֶץ.

שִׁשָּׁה מִי יוֹדֵעַ? שִׁשָּׁה אֲנִי יוֹדֵעַ: שִׁשָּׁה סִדְרֵי מִשְׁנָה, חֲמִשָּׁה חוּמְשֵׁי תוֹרָה, אַרְבַּע אִמָּהוֹת, שְׁלֹשָׁה אָבוֹת, שְׁנֵי לֻחוֹת הַבְּרִית, אֶחָד אֱלֹהֵינוּ שֶׁבַּשָּׁמַיִם וּבָאָרֶץ.

שִׁבְעָה מִי יוֹדֵעַ? שִׁבְעָה אֲנִי יוֹדֵעַ: שִׁבְעָה יְמֵי שַׁבָּתָא, שִׁשָּׁה סִדְרֵי מִשְׁנָה, חֲמִשָּׁה חוּמְשֵׁי תוֹרָה, אַרְבַּע אִמָּהוֹת, שְׁלֹשָׁה אָבוֹת, שְׁנֵי לֻחוֹת הַבְּרִית, אֶחָד אֱלֹהֵינוּ שֶׁבַּשָּׁמַיִם וּבָאָרֶץ.

שְׁמוֹנָה מִי יוֹדֵעַ? שְׁמוֹנָה אֲנִי יוֹדֵעַ: שְׁמוֹנָה יְמֵי מִילָה, שִׁבְעָה יְמֵי שַׁבָּתָא, שִׁשָּׁה סִדְרֵי מִשְׁנָה, חֲמִשָּׁה חוּמְשֵׁי תוֹרָה, אַרְבַּע אִמָּהוֹת, שְׁלֹשָׁה אָבוֹת, שְׁנֵי לֻחוֹת הַבְּרִית, אֶחָד אֱלֹהֵינוּ שֶׁבַּשָּׁמַיִם וּבָאָרֶץ.

Who knows ten?
I know ten. Ten are the Ten Commandments.

Who knows eleven?
I know eleven. Eleven are the stars in Joseph's dream.

Who knows twelve?
I know twelve. Twelve are the tribes of Israel.

Who knows thirteen?
I know thirteen. Thirteen are the attributes of God.
Twelve are the tribes of Israel.
Eleven are the stars in Joseph's dream.
Ten are the Ten Commandments.
Nine are the months of pregnancy.
Eight are the days until brit milah.
Seven are the days of the week.
Six are the books of the Mishnah.
Five are the books of the Torah.
Four are the mamas.
Three are the papas.
Two are the tablets that Moshe brought.
One is our God, one is our God, one is our God—in the heavens and the earth.

תִּשְׁעָה מִי יוֹדֵעַ? תִּשְׁעָה אֲנִי יוֹדֵעַ: תִּשְׁעָה יַרְחֵי לֵדָה, שְׁמוֹנָה יְמֵי מִילָה, שִׁבְעָה יְמֵי שַׁבַּתָּא, שִׁשָּׁה סִדְרֵי מִשְׁנָה, חֲמִשָּׁה חוּמְשֵׁי תוֹרָה, אַרְבַּע אִמָּהוֹת, שְׁלֹשָׁה אָבוֹת, שְׁנֵי לֻחוֹת הַבְּרִית, אֶחָד אֱלֹהֵינוּ שֶׁבַּשָּׁמַיִם וּבָאָרֶץ.

עֲשָׂרָה מִי יוֹדֵעַ? עֲשָׂרָה אֲנִי יוֹדֵעַ: עֲשָׂרָה דִבְּרַיָא, תִּשְׁעָה יַרְחֵי לֵדָה, שְׁמוֹנָה יְמֵי מִילָה, שִׁבְעָה יְמֵי שַׁבַּתָּא, שִׁשָּׁה סִדְרֵי מִשְׁנָה, חֲמִשָּׁה חוּמְשֵׁי תוֹרָה, אַרְבַּע אִמָּהוֹת, שְׁלֹשָׁה אָבוֹת, שְׁנֵי לֻחוֹת הַבְּרִית, אֶחָד אֱלֹהֵינוּ שֶׁבַּשָּׁמַיִם וּבָאָרֶץ.

אַחַד עָשָׂר מִי יוֹדֵעַ? אַחַד עָשָׂר אֲנִי יוֹדֵעַ: אַחַד עָשָׂר כּוֹכְבַיָא, עֲשָׂרָה דִבְּרַיָא, תִּשְׁעָה יַרְחֵי לֵדָה, שְׁמוֹנָה יְמֵי מִילָה, שִׁבְעָה יְמֵי שַׁבַּתָּא, שִׁשָּׁה סִדְרֵי מִשְׁנָה, חֲמִשָּׁה חוּמְשֵׁי תוֹרָה, אַרְבַּע אִמָּהוֹת, שְׁלֹשָׁה אָבוֹת, שְׁנֵי לֻחוֹת הַבְּרִית, אֶחָד אֱלֹהֵינוּ שֶׁבַּשָּׁמַיִם וּבָאָרֶץ.

שְׁנֵים עָשָׂר מִי יוֹדֵעַ? שְׁנֵים עָשָׂר אֲנִי יוֹדֵעַ: שְׁנֵים עָשָׂר שִׁבְטַיָא, אַחַד עָשָׂר כּוֹכְבַיָא, עֲשָׂרָה דִבְּרַיָא, תִּשְׁעָה יַרְחֵי לֵדָה, שְׁמוֹנָה יְמֵי מִילָה, שִׁבְעָה יְמֵי שַׁבַּתָּא, שִׁשָּׁה סִדְרֵי מִשְׁנָה, חֲמִשָּׁה חוּמְשֵׁי תוֹרָה, אַרְבַּע אִמָּהוֹת, שְׁלֹשָׁה אָבוֹת, שְׁנֵי לֻחוֹת הַבְּרִית, אֶחָד אֱלֹהֵינוּ שֶׁבַּשָּׁמַיִם וּבָאָרֶץ.

שְׁלֹשָׁה עָשָׂר מִי יוֹדֵעַ? שְׁלֹשָׁה עָשָׂר אֲנִי יוֹדֵעַ: שְׁלֹשָׁה עָשָׂר מִדַּיָא. שְׁנֵים עָשָׂר שִׁבְטַיָא, אַחַד עָשָׂר כּוֹכְבַיָא, עֲשָׂרָה דִבְּרַיָא, תִּשְׁעָה יַרְחֵי לֵדָה, שְׁמוֹנָה יְמֵי מִילָה, שִׁבְעָה יְמֵי שַׁבַּתָּא, שִׁשָּׁה סִדְרֵי מִשְׁנָה, חֲמִשָּׁה חוּמְשֵׁי תוֹרָה, אַרְבַּע אִמָּהוֹת, שְׁלֹשָׁה אָבוֹת, שְׁנֵי לֻחוֹת הַבְּרִית, אֶחָד אֱלֹהֵינוּ שֶׁבַּשָּׁמַיִם וּבָאָרֶץ.

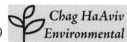
Chag HaAviv
Environmental

Chag HaPesach
Storytelling

Chag HaCheirut
Liberation

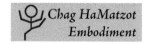
Chag HaMatzot
Embodiment

Adir Hu   אַדִּיר הוּא

Adir hu yivneh beito b'karov.
El benei, el benei, benei beitcha
b'karov.

Mighty is God. May God
build God's house soon. Quickly,
quickly, in our days, soon. God
build, God build, build Your
house soon.

Chosen is God, great is God,
noted is God. May God...

Decorated is God,
distinguished is God,
meritorious is God. May God...

Pious is God, pure is God,
unique is God. May God...

Powerful is God, learned is
God, a king is God. May God...

Intense is God, exalted is God,
heroic is God. May God...

A restorer is God, righteous is
God, holy is God. May God...

Nurturing is God, the one who
holds enough is God, dynamic is
God. May God...

אַדִּיר הוּא יִבְנֶה בֵּיתוֹ בְּקָרוֹב. בִּמְהֵרָה, בִּמְהֵרָה, בְּיָמֵינוּ בְּקָרוֹב. אֵל בְּנֵה, אֵל בְּנֵה, בְּנֵה בֵיתְךָ בְּקָרוֹב.

בָּחוּר הוּא, גָּדוֹל הוּא, דָּגוּל הוּא יִבְנֶה בֵּיתוֹ בְּקָרוֹב. בִּמְהֵרָה, בִּמְהֵרָה, בְּיָמֵינוּ בְּקָרוֹב. אֵל בְּנֵה, אֵל בְּנֵה, בְּנֵה בֵיתְךָ בְּקָרוֹב.

הָדוּר הוּא, וָתִיק הוּא, זַכַּאי הוּא יִבְנֶה בֵּיתוֹ בְּקָרוֹב. בִּמְהֵרָה, בִּמְהֵרָה, בְּיָמֵינוּ בְּקָרוֹב. אֵל בְּנֵה, אֵל בְּנֵה, בְּנֵה בֵיתְךָ בְּקָרוֹב.

חָסִיד הוּא, טָהוֹר הוּא, יָחִיד הוּא יִבְנֶה בֵּיתוֹ בְּקָרוֹב. בִּמְהֵרָה, בִּמְהֵרָה, בְּיָמֵינוּ בְּקָרוֹב. אֵל בְּנֵה, אֵל בְּנֵה, בְּנֵה בֵיתְךָ בְּקָרוֹב.

כַּבִּיר הוּא, לָמוּד הוּא, מֶלֶךְ הוּא יִבְנֶה בֵּיתוֹ בְּקָרוֹב. בִּמְהֵרָה, בִּמְהֵרָה, בְּיָמֵינוּ בְּקָרוֹב. אֵל בְּנֵה, אֵל בְּנֵה, בְּנֵה בֵיתְךָ בְּקָרוֹב.

נוֹרָא הוּא, סַגִּיב הוּא, עִזּוּז הוּא יִבְנֶה בֵּיתוֹ בְּקָרוֹב. בִּמְהֵרָה, בִּמְהֵרָה, בְּיָמֵינוּ בְּקָרוֹב. אֵל בְּנֵה, אֵל בְּנֵה, בְּנֵה בֵיתְךָ בְּקָרוֹב.

פּוֹדֶה הוּא, צַדִּיק הוּא, קָדוֹשׁ הוּא יִבְנֶה בֵּיתוֹ בְּקָרוֹב. בִּמְהֵרָה, בִּמְהֵרָה, בְּיָמֵינוּ בְּקָרוֹב. אֵל בְּנֵה, אֵל בְּנֵה, בְּנֵה בֵיתְךָ בְּקָרוֹב.

רַחוּם הוּא, שַׁדַּי הוּא, תַּקִּיף הוּא יִבְנֶה בֵּיתוֹ בְּקָרוֹב. בִּמְהֵרָה, בִּמְהֵרָה, בְּיָמֵינוּ בְּקָרוֹב. אֵל בְּנֵה, אֵל בְּנֵה, בְּנֵה בֵיתְךָ בְּקָרוֹב.

Ki Lo Na'eh

*Lecha u'lecha, lecha ki lecha, lecha
Adonai hamamlecha.
Ki lo na'eh, ki lo ya'eh.*

Mighty in authority, chosen
according to the way, God's
troops shall say to God, "Yours
and Yours, Yours since it is Yours,
Yours and even Yours, Yours,
Lord is the kingdom; since for
God it is pleasant, for God it is
suited."

Noted in authority, splendid
according to the way, God's
seniors say, "Yours..."

Meritorious in authority, robust
according to the way, God's
scribes say, "Yours..."

Unique in authority, powerful
according to the way, God's
scholars say, "Yours..."

Reigning in authority, intense
according to the way, those
surrounding say, "Yours..."

Humble in authority, restoring
according to the way, God's
righteous say, "Yours..."

Holy in authority, nurturing
according to the way, God's
angels' say, "Yours..."

Dynamic in authority, supportive
according to the way, God's whole
ones say, "Yours..."

כִּי לוֹ נָאֶה, כִּי לוֹ יָאֶה

אַדִּיר בִּמְלוּכָה, בָּחוּר כַּהֲלָכָה, גְּדוּדָיו יֹאמְרוּ
לוֹ: לְךָ וּלְךָ, לְךָ כִּי לְךָ, לְךָ אַף לְךָ, לְךָ ה'
הַמַּמְלָכָה, כִּי לוֹ נָאֶה, כִּי לוֹ יָאֶה.
דָּגוּל בִּמְלוּכָה, הָדוּר כַּהֲלָכָה, וָתִיקָיו יֹאמְרוּ
לוֹ: לְךָ וּלְךָ, לְךָ כִּי לְךָ, לְךָ אַף לְךָ, לְךָ ה'
הַמַּמְלָכָה, כִּי לוֹ נָאֶה, כִּי לוֹ יָאֶה.
זַכַּאי בִּמְלוּכָה, חָסִין כַּהֲלָכָה טַפְסְרָיו יֹאמְרוּ
לוֹ: לְךָ וּלְךָ, לְךָ כִּי לְךָ, לְךָ אַף לְךָ, לְךָ ה'
הַמַּמְלָכָה, כִּי לוֹ נָאֶה, כִּי לוֹ יָאֶה.
יָחִיד בִּמְלוּכָה, כַּבִּיר כַּהֲלָכָה לִמּוּדָיו יֹאמְרוּ
לוֹ: לְךָ וּלְךָ, לְךָ כִּי לְךָ, לְךָ אַף לְךָ, לְךָ ה'
הַמַּמְלָכָה, כִּי לוֹ נָאֶה, כִּי לוֹ יָאֶה.
מוֹשֵׁל בִּמְלוּכָה, נוֹרָא כַּהֲלָכָה סְבִיבָיו יֹאמְרוּ
לוֹ: לְךָ וּלְךָ, לְךָ כִּי לְךָ, לְךָ אַף לְךָ, לְךָ ה'
הַמַּמְלָכָה, כִּי לוֹ נָאֶה, כִּי לוֹ יָאֶה.
עָנָיו בִּמְלוּכָה, פּוֹדֶה כַּהֲלָכָה, צַדִּיקָיו יֹאמְרוּ
לוֹ: לְךָ וּלְךָ, לְךָ כִּי לְךָ, לְךָ אַף לְךָ, לְךָ ה'
הַמַּמְלָכָה, כִּי לוֹ נָאֶה, כִּי לוֹ יָאֶה.
קָדוֹשׁ בִּמְלוּכָה, רַחוּם כַּהֲלָכָה שִׁנְאַנָּיו יֹאמְרוּ
לוֹ: לְךָ וּלְךָ, לְךָ כִּי לְךָ, לְךָ אַף לְךָ, לְךָ ה'
הַמַּמְלָכָה, כִּי לוֹ נָאֶה, כִּי לוֹ יָאֶה.
תַּקִּיף בִּמְלוּכָה, תּוֹמֵךְ כַּהֲלָכָה תְּמִימָיו יֹאמְרוּ
לוֹ: לְךָ וּלְךָ, לְךָ כִּי לְךָ, לְךָ אַף לְךָ, לְךָ ה'
הַמַּמְלָכָה, כִּי לוֹ נָאֶה, כִּי לוֹ יָאֶה.

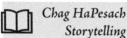
Chag HaAviv
Environmental

Chag HaPesach
Storytelling

Chag HaCheirut
Liberation

Chag HaMatzot
Embodiment

Chad Gadya

Chad gadya, chad gadya. Dzabin Abba bitrei zuzei, chad gadya, chad gadya.

One little kid, one little kid that my father bought for two *zuz*, one kid, one kid.
Then came a cat and ate the kid...

Then came a dog and bit the cat, that ate the kid...

Then came a stick and hit the dog, that bit the cat, that ate the kid...

Then came fire and burnt the stick, that hit the dog, that bit the cat, that ate the kid...

Then came water and extinguished the fire, that burnt the stick, that hit the dog, that bit the cat, that ate the kid...

Then came an ox and drank the water, that extinguished the fire, that burnt the stick, that hit the dog, that bit the cat, that ate the kid...

Then came the butcher and slaughtered the ox, that drank the water, that extinguished the fire, that burnt the stick, that hit the dog, that bit the cat, that ate the kid...

חַד גַּדְיָא

חַד גַּדְיָא, חַד גַּדְיָא דְּזַבִּין אַבָּא
בִּתְרֵי זוּזֵי, חַד גַּדְיָא, חַד גַּדְיָא.
וְאָתָא שׁוּנְרָא וְאָכְלָה לְגַדְיָא, דְּזַבִּין
אַבָּא בִּתְרֵי זוּזֵי. חַד גַּדְיָא, חַד גַּדְיָא.
וְאָתָא כַלְבָּא וְנָשַׁךְ לְשׁוּנְרָא, דְּאָכְלָה
לְגַדְיָא, דְּזַבִּין אַבָּא בִּתְרֵי זוּזֵי. חַד
גַּדְיָא, חַד גַּדְיָא.
וְאָתָא חוּטְרָא וְהִכָּה לְכַלְבָּא, דְּנָשַׁךְ
לְשׁוּנְרָא, דְּאָכְלָה לְגַדְיָא, דְּזַבִּין אַבָּא
בִּתְרֵי זוּזֵי. חַד גַּדְיָא, חַד גַּדְיָא.
וְאָתָא נוּרָא וְשָׂרַף לְחוּטְרָא, דְּהִכָּה
לְכַלְבָּא, דְּנָשַׁךְ לְשׁוּנְרָא, דְּאָכְלָה
לְגַדְיָא, דְּזַבִּין אַבָּא בִּתְרֵי זוּזֵי. חַד
גַּדְיָא, חַד גַּדְיָא.
וְאָתָא מַיָּא וְכָבָה לְנוּרָא, דְּשָׂרַף
לְחוּטְרָא, דְּהִכָּה לְכַלְבָּא, דְּנָשַׁךְ
לְשׁוּנְרָא, דְּאָכְלָה לְגַדְיָא, דְּזַבִּין אַבָּא
בִּתְרֵי זוּזֵי. חַד גַּדְיָא, חַד גַּדְיָא.
וְאָתָא תוֹרָא וְשָׁתָה לְמַיָּא, דְּכָבָה
לְנוּרָא, דְּשָׂרַף לְחוּטְרָא, דְּהִכָּה
לְכַלְבָּא, דְּנָשַׁךְ לְשׁוּנְרָא, דְּאָכְלָה
לְגַדְיָא, דְּזַבִּין אַבָּא בִּתְרֵי זוּזֵי. חַד
גַּדְיָא, חַד גַּדְיָא.
וְאָתָא הַשּׁוֹחֵט וְשָׁחַט לְתוֹרָא, דְּשָׁתָה
לְמַיָּא, דְּכָבָה לְנוּרָא, דְּשָׂרַף לְחוּטְרָא,
דְּהִכָּה לְכַלְבָּא, דְּנָשַׁךְ לְשׁוּנְרָא,
דְּאָכְלָה לְגַדְיָא, דְּזַבִּין אַבָּא בִּתְרֵי זוּזֵי.
חַד גַּדְיָא, חַד גַּדְיָא.

Then came the angel of death and slaughtered the schochet, who slaughtered the bull, that drank the water, that extinguished the fire, that burnt the stick, that hit the dog, that bit the cat, that ate the kid...

Then came the Holy Blessed One and slaughtered the angel of death, who slaughtered the schochet, who slaughtered the bull, that drank the water, that extinguished the fire, that burnt the stick, that hit the dog, that bit the cat, that ate the kid that my father bought for two zuz, one kid, one kid.

וְאָתָא מַלְאַךְ הַמָּוֶת וְשָׁחַט לְשׁוֹחֵט, דְּשָׁחַט לְתוֹרָא, דְּשָׁתָה לְמַיָּא, דְּכָבָה לְנוּרָא, דְּשָׂרַף לְחוּטְרָא, דְּהִכָּה לְכַלְבָּא, דְּנָשַׁךְ לְשׁוּנְרָא, דְּאָכְלָה לְגַדְיָא, דְּזַבִּין אַבָּא בִּתְרֵי זוּזֵי. חַד גַּדְיָא, חַד גַּדְיָא.

וְאָתָא הַקָּדוֹשׁ בָּרוּךְ הוּא וְשָׁחַט לְמַלְאַךְ הַמָּוֶת, דְּשָׁחַט לְשׁוֹחֵט, דְּשָׁחַט לְתוֹרָא, דְּשָׁתָה לְמַיָּא, דְּכָבָה לְנוּרָא, דְּשָׂרַף לְחוּטְרָא, דְּהִכָּה לְכַלְבָּא, דְּנָשַׁךְ לְשׁוּנְרָא, דְּאָכְלָה לְגַדְיָא, דְּזַבִּין אַבָּא בִּתְרֵי זוּזֵי. חַד גַּדְיָא, חַד גַּדְיָא.

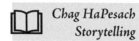
Chag HaAviv
Environmental

Chag HaPesach
Storytelling

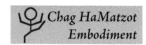
Chag HaCheirut
Liberation

Chag HaMatzot
Embodiment

Completed is the Seder of Pesach according to its law, according to all its judgement and statute. Just as we have merited to arrange it, so too, may we merit to do [its sacrifice]. Pure One who dwells in the habitation, raise up the congregation of the community, which whom can count. Bring close, lead the plantings of the sapling, redeemed, to Zion in joy.

Next year, let us be in the built Jerusalem!

חֲסַל סִדּוּר פֶּסַח כְּהִלְכָתוֹ, כְּכָל מִשְׁפָּטוֹ וְחֻקָּתוֹ. כַּאֲשֶׁר זָכִינוּ לְסַדֵּר אוֹתוֹ כֵּן נִזְכֶּה לַעֲשׂוֹתוֹ. זָךְ שׁוֹכֵן מְעוֹנָה, קוֹמֵם קְהַל עֲדַת מִי מָנָה. בְּקָרוֹב נַהֵל נִטְעֵי כַנָּה פְּדוּיִם לְצִיּוֹן בְּרִנָּה.

לְשָׁנָה הַבָּאָה בִּירוּשָׁלַיִם הַבְּנוּיָה.

Acknowledgements And Gratitude

The Hebrew typeset used for the Haggadah text is Mazon, created by Noemi Lasalandra. Thank you Noemi!

I have, at times, expressed jealousy for my musician friends who make art in bands and groups. Visual arts can feel lonely and isolated at times. The experience of writing music for someone else to play has always appealed to me (in theory—that is very much not my skillset). However, this isn't truly fair or representative of the way this Haggadah has come into the world. I am grateful to so many others who have supported and guided me.

I am blessed and honored to be a queer Jew in a moment in history where I can lean into the fullness of both of those identities. I come from deep, old traditions that are still evolving and growing. I am so grateful to all of my ancestors, and to everyone who has kept those traditions alive, and everyone who has worked to uncover and rediscover history that was lost or repressed. This work has grown alongside a study of Jewish world history project as well as ongoing research into queer history and culture. I am so grateful to the historians, archivists, and translators who have made my roots available to me. I am also appreciative of the scientists, naturalists, and Indigenous folks who have shaped my understanding of the natural world and its beauty, complexity, and fragility.

I would like to thank Larry Yudelson at Ben Yehuda Press for taking my cold email and running with it. Our conversations have been a joy. I'm so glad and honored that my Haggadah has a home alongside the other work you publish. Thank you to Bogi Takács for their insightful and helpful comments and edits. Thank you to Rachel Jackson for invaluable feedback on graphic design. Thanks to Joe Buchwald Gelles and Bear Bergman who patiently answered my questions about publishing early in the process.

This Haggadah would not have been possible without the resources made available by Sefaria. I used their text and tweaked their translation. The vast majority of my research into Jewish texts and sources was made possible by their user-friendly format. Thank you for all you do for the Jewish people.

Thank you to so many friends and relations for their enthusiasm and support, and for allowing me to talk about Passover year-round. Thank you to Molly Moses for our periodic art dates. We should do more of that. Thanks to Rabbi Leora Abelson for ongoing support, encouragement, and challenge—both about the Haggadah and generally. Thanks to Emily Fishman for detailed and thoughtful feedback. Althea Pestine, Bobby Stevens, Anne Johnston, and Robert Johnston joined Sandy and me for seder in 2021 using a very early draft of this Haggadah. That experience

was invaluable. I'm grateful to Anne Johnston for her constant support of me as an artist and a Jewish artist. Thanks to Robert Johnston for his insightful questions and historical perspective, and for embracing my queerness from day one.

Some of the art in this haggadah was created in my grandfather's hospice room at Evelyn's House in St. Louis, Missouri. Thank you to Grandpa for welcoming me into that space and to the staff who supported my whole family during fall 2022. I miss you and I love you, Grandpa.

My siblings have provided support and feedback. Thank you to Isaac Johnston for your support and challenge. Thank you to Rabbi Rafi Spitzer for thoughts, feedback, comments, questions, and ongoing support. I appreciate how intentional you are about making time for family, including me, and for always showing up. Thank you to Arielle for your feedback on the early draft of the Haggadah, including your suggestions on how a seder leader could use the four voices. Thank you to Leora for challenging me to actually get started on this project, and for providing constant feedback and serious (and lighthearted) discussions. It is a joy and a blessing to discuss queer yiddishkeyt with you.

I'm incredibly privileged to have been raised immersed in the depth and breadth Jewish tradition, text, and culture. Thank you to my parents for having excellent seders growing up, and to everyone over the years who attended them. Thank you to my mother my teacher Rabbi Miriam Spitzer for her thoughtful comments on the Haggadah and constant modeling of what it means to take Judaism seriously, critically, and with integrity. Thank you to my father my teacher Jeffrey Spitzer for teaching me to love Talmud and that the entire library of Jewish text is my inheritance and can be available to me. I have found studying Jewish texts challenging in any number of ways, but I have never been intimidated by seforim. Thank you to both my parents for building that foundation for me.

To Sandy, my life chavruta, it is a blessing to grow with you. Thank you for all of your support as I have balanced this project with a full-time job and various volunteer commitments. You challenge me and make me sharper and stronger every day. And you balance that with patience, kindness, softness, and silliness. Thank you for setting such a high bar. I love you.

Artwork by Page

Art may be available as prints. Contact the artist at www.GabriellaSpitzer.com.

Citations and References, by Page

vi: Rabbi Leora Abelson Yom Kippur sermon reprinted with permission of the author.

vii: Credit to Laynie Solomon's excellent essay "Halakha Beyond the Binary" https://svara.org/halakha-beyond-the-binary/

5: From Women on Nature, ed. Kathrine Norbury. Used with permission of the author.

8: Quotation from Braiding Sweetgrass used with permission of the publisher, Milkweed Editions.

9: Questions for Google used with permission of the author.

15: Used with permission. Copyright Dar Williams "You're Aging Well" 1994 Burningfield Music.

21: From WHAT IS FOUND THERE: Notebooks on Poetry and Politics by Adrienne Rich. Copyright ©1993 by Adrienne Rich. Used by permission of W. W. Norton & Company, Inc.

22: Excerpt(s) from FINDING THE MOTHER TREE: DISCOVERING THE WISDOM OF THE FOREST by Suzanne Simard, copyright © 2021 by Suzanne Simard. Used by permission of Alfred A. Knopf, an imprint of the Knopf Doubleday Publishing Group, a division of Penguin Random House LLC. All rights reserved.

24: Time Passes used with permission of the author.

25: Used with permission from the publisher.

27: Many thanks for Rabbi Aryeh Bernstein from making me aware of these sources in his remarkable essay "The Torah Case for Reparations" https://aryehbernstein.medium.com/the-torah-case-for-reparations-bbe41e7763c0

31: Translation by Aviva Ben Ur reprinted with permission of the translator.

35: From Undrowned by Alexis Pauline Gumbs. Used with permission of AK Press.

36: From Pilgrim at Tinker Creek by Annie Dillard. Copyright © 1974 by Annie Dillard. Used by permission of HarperCollins Publishers.

38: Tzipporah: Exodus 4:22-26 by Alana Suskin used with permission of the author.

39: Translation from the Ladino by Dina Danon as printed in Sephardi Lives, Stanford University Press.

48: Thank you to Leora Spitzer for the comments about Pharaoh's deputies doing the dirty work.

49: Many thanks to Avigayil Halpern for the insight into collective punishment and the captive in the dungeon.

56: Many thanks to Rabbi Rafi Spitzer, Leora Spitzer, and Lexie Botzum for their insights into the meaning of Dayenu.

57-60: I am indebted to so many Jewish feminist liturgists for their part growing the traditional text of the Haggadah to include Miriam's voice. Specific appreciation goes to Jamie Schwartz's Sefaria sourcesheets that pointed me to many of these sources.